Praise

"Unlikely to Unstoppable: Success Stories from Everyday Entrepreneurs by Jennifer Collins and Elizabeth Clark is an enlightening collection of the real-life stories of thirteen individuals who achieved success by taking roads less traveled. Fundamental principles of steadfast determination, perseverance, and flexibility are highlighted. . . .

"[This book] is an unrivaled source of motivation. It will be a useful tool for anyone who is unclear of their course or who thinks—or has been told—that their goals are impossible. Its grounded tone and relatable content will appeal to a broader range of people of all ages and educational backgrounds. Its documentary-like storytelling and realistic tone, along with a smooth, analytical, and thoughtful approach, beautifully distinguish it from other books." – Lily Andrews, Reader Views

"This thought-provoking and inspiring read offers insight into the lives of thirteen 'everyday entrepreneurs.' The stories of hard-working people who do well for themselves provide opportunities for even an experienced individual to learn something new.

"The story of one of the thirteen, now the owner of a painting business, who was a self-proclaimed goofball in high school, illustrates the central theme of the book. Although nothing came easy for him, he struggled toward his goals with undiluted grit. His journey embodies this message: go for it, and *never, ever* take no for an answer.

"If you want to make it as an entrepreneur and you don't know where to start, check out this book. Like the go-getters featured in Unlikely to Unstoppable, you just have to battle on." –A Wishing Shelf Book Review

"I found myself furiously writing down theories, ideas, words, meanings while I read . . . not that all the concepts were original or unique, however this book is FULL; full of pearls, of knowledge, experiences, raw emotions, and moments I want to share when I teach, when I lead, and when I mentor. I truly cannot wait to read it again.

"After having read so many of the classics on leadership, success, and motivation, *Unlikely to Unstoppable* is a stand-out combining the research methodology that appeals to the academic with the focused storytelling that appeals to the entrepreneur! It made me pause to evaluate my own definition of success—isn't that all you wish to achieve as an author, the engagement of your readers? A real gem in encouraging introspection and critical thinking!" –Denise Cavanaugh, EdD, Academic Coach, Business Instructor, Entrepreneur/Business Owner

"What are the critical elements for success? Passion, Persistence, and knowing when to Pivot are but a few of the ingredients shared in a book full of entrepreneurial wisdom, told from the vantage point of the success-story-next-door. Authors Collins and Clark remind us that each and every one of us has an opportunity to be unstoppable!

"What differentiates this book from the many leadership tomes is that the authors distill the key ingredients of entrepreneurship, not from the rich and famous but from the journeys of thirteen 'people next door.' Thoughtful and compelling, this book reminds us that we all have the potential to be unstoppable.

"There are many pearls of entrepreneurial wisdom in this book; the main one being that there is no one, definitive path, no 'right way that leads to success. What you will learn, though, is that Ted Collins, "Doc Lilac," was a remarkable man, and his story along with those of twelve other remarkable business people, will inspire you and provide tips to embark on your own unique unstoppable journey." –Angela Rosenberg, DrPH, Leadership Consultant, and Author of the Enneagram in Nature series

UNLIKELY

TO

UNSTOPPABLE

Stories
from Everyday
Entrepreneurs

Jennifer Collins
Elizabeth Clark

Unlikely to Unstoppable: Stories from Everyday Entrepreneurs

Jennifer Collins and Elizabeth Clark

Publisher: Words in the Wings Press, Inc.
2366 Turk Hill Rd., Victor, NY 14564
Contact: wordsinthewings2021@gmail.com

979-8-9985387-0-4 Hardcover

979-8-9985387-1-1 Paperback

979-8-9985387-2-8 Electronic Book

Library of Congress Control Number: 2025907446

Publisher's Cataloging-in-Publication Data

Names: Collins, Jennifer E., author. | Clark, Elizabeth M., author.

Title: Unlikely to unstoppable : stories from everyday entrepreneurs / Jennifer Collins and Elizabeth Clark.

Description: Includes bibliographical references. | Victor, NY: Words in the Wings Press, Inc., 2025.

Identifiers: LCCN: 2025907446 | ISBN: 979-8-9985387-0-4 (hardcover) | 979-8-9985387-1-1 (paperback) | 979-8-9985387-2-8 (ebook)

Subjects: LCSH Entrepreneurship. | Entrepreneurship--Case studies. | Businesspeople--Anecdotes. | Business enterprises. | Success in business.| BISAC BUSINESS & ECONOMICS / Entrepreneurship | BUSINESS & ECONOMICS / Motivational | BUSINESS & ECONOMICS / Personal Success | SELF-HELP / Motivational & Inspirational

Classification: LCC HC102.5.A2 .C65 2025 | DDC 658.4/09--dc23

*To all of the inspiring people I've been
privileged to know: patients, students, colleagues, friends, and family members.
My love for you is unstoppable,
Jenny*

*This book is dedicated to YOU!
Be encouraged and inspired to live outside
your comfort zone . . . for that is where all
of the magic exists.
XO, Eliz*

Credits

Cover Photography: Ed Dobrowski
Cover Design: Sarah Maxwell and MediaNeighbours
Editing and Interior Design: Mary Neighbour
Author Photo: Photography by Anna

Contents

Preface

We encounter people multiple times a day—at work, at the grocery store, on the subway. Often these are brief contacts: a glance as you hold the door for someone behind you, a nod to a stranger to let them pass you in the aisle, a smile from another passenger on a long ride home. Some of these meetings evolve into conversations, but how is it that with over eight billion people on earth, only a small fraction of a percentage become individuals you talk to? Are you ever curious about people's stories? Where did they come from and where are they going? Might they have a shared path or a message that aligns with your journey? Countless opportunities to listen, learn, and incorporate others' lessons into our daily lives are likely escaping us.

That is a little bit of what this book is all about, a series of stories to introduce thirteen people, strangers to you at this moment. Each has carved their own way to success with some combination of "luck," and a lot of hard work. They are trailblazers in many ways, willing to share their stories of finding a way and open to making connections with willing listeners. Their stories are filled with hidden gems, mined from our curiosity to hear more.

While common practice is to classify a book as a particular genre, this one is a bit like a square peg in a round hole! Biography, memoir, self-help, creative nonfiction. It does not precisely fit under any of these labels. At once a product of research, a compendium of first-person story-telling, and even a work of admiration and love, this book leaps over genres—a single label is elusive.

By whatever name, this compilation, featuring the words of thirteen individuals, began with one person as a specific inspiration. The driving force originated from experiences of knowing a man named Ted and the authors' questions about whether there was something unique about him, his upbringing, his attitudes, or some other yet-to-be-identified "thing," that led to his interesting life. That inkling led us to seek out others who also appeared to march to the beat of their own drum, who found reward-ing vocations, even success, in spite of somewhat unlikely beginnings. Those who forged their way along less-traveled paths. People we've come to think of as everyday entrepre-neurs. Ultimately, we offer a collection of stories that may inspire your own ongoing efforts to navigate life's highway.

The project began with the idea to learn more about people who, in spite of unlikely circumstances, whether by virtue of upbringing, education, or even a passion for a field typically predominated by people unlike them—differ-ent genders, different socioeconomic status, whatever—remained steadfast in their efforts to achieve their goals and pursue their dreams. People who did not necessarily blindly follow the path recommended by well-meaning parents, advisors, or school officials. Individuals who stumbled upon a career that even they didn't necessarily expect. Ted was such a person, leading life his own way, on his own terms.

The authors had previous experience with inter-view research in the academic setting. In academics, identification of suitable research projects aimed at publication reigns supreme. Investigating people who seemed in some way similar to Ted would be different, less scientific, and more personal. This inquiry was led by a desire to listen and learn about the individual first. Finding similarities to what we knew about Ted came next. Thoughts of writing and publishing were last. It was a fresh, untrodden journey for us, allowing each author to examine, for the pure sake of understanding, unlikely individuals on intriguing paths.

As we roamed, uncertain of our destination, we relied upon the skills we had mastered previously: developing questions, recruiting people, and structuring interviews, giving deliberate attention to ensuring each person was asked the same things so that comparisons could later be made. We then embarked upon hours and hours of listening to tales of failures, circuitous paths, or changed goals from the perspectives of people who lived through those ups and downs. The storytellers willingly poured out their hopes, dreams, and disappointments.

Interviewing these folks not only held the authors' own interest but raised questions as to whether their words might also intrigue others. Witnessing the storytelling was a true privilege, and it soon became apparent that our interviews were destined to become a combined narrative. The stories were sprinkled with laughter, tears, enthusiastic hand gestures, and more than a few "a-ha" moments for both the interviewers and the interviewees. Along the way, we encountered suggestions for other interesting candidates, and ultimately, we realized our project could have easily expanded to include dozens more. But once the authors took pause and began analyzing the transcripts for consistent themes, it was apparent that similarities across the storytellers did already exist. Commonalities that stood out despite them being dissimilar in demographic characteristics, background descriptors, and field or business.

More interviews and more stories were not necessary after all. The recorded words already articulated fascinating ideas. Ideas with the potential to debunk commonly-held beliefs. The people interviewed had incredibly valuable messages of hope, persistence, and a "can-do" attitude that deserved to be captured and passed along to others.

Admittedly, we collected a mélange of storytelling styles, sometimes chatty, other times quite analytical. And in writing these stories, we aimed to stay true to the voice of each interviewee. We also wove in our own expertise, and so this book is rooted in qualitative research and has value as a study of concepts such as work, success, and entrepreneurialism. Its testimonials and quotes will be motivational for readers who do not wish to select the traditional academic route in pursuit of their dreams, who want to follow their own inclinations of fulfillment and success, or who are now questioning where in their own lives to begin. A page titled "Notes to Self" is included at the back of the book to give such readers a place to brainstorm their own potential journeys. In sum, this book will appeal to readers who simply enjoy a well-told, charming story, with reassurance to follow their own direction in life.

Finally, it is a nod of respect for the lives of many who choose an unlikely or unexpected path, especially those we were fortunate to meet along the way. May these firsthand stories captivate you and bring moments of reflection and introspection.

Introduction to Our "Unlikely" Contributors

"Unlikely"—alone, this word does not necessarily portray a flattering description. The word literally means *not likely*, or *not probable*. However, when paired with "Unstoppable," it is intended to express an admiration for those being featured. People best characterized as starting from one place, with or without a plan, and continuing to move forward despite obstacles in their paths.

"Unlikely to Unstoppable" is meant to pique your interest and raise curiosity. What comes to mind when thinking of someone who is *unlikely* to do something? A person who performs outside of typical expectations or whose accomplishments are considered improbable. To categorize someone as unlikely, there must be a perceived expectation of what is likely.

For example, there is a standard for compulsory education in the United States. School is required through grade twelve. A high school diploma is often the entry-level criteria for employment. Therefore, attending and finishing high school is the *likely* or expected route traversed by most young people. Superlative awards are often a rite of passage in high school, recognizing such qualities as "best team player," "funniest," or "most stylish." One common award in particular highlights the concept of *likely*—the one titled "Most Likely to Succeed." This accolade seemingly recognizes skills such as commitment, drive, excellence, and leadership. It also suggests that someone "unlikely to succeed" would be the opposite.

A related belief in modern society is that not only is a high school diploma expected, but education beyond high school is necessary to attain rewarding careers. And some ascribe to the assumption that the more education the better. This is captured in the concept of Human Capital Theory (Becker, 1975). Becker posits that education determines one's productivity, and consequently, earnings. Therefore, the way to elevate oneself in a society that endorses this idea is to succeed in higher education. However, in recent years, the costs of higher education have sky-rocketed—not to mention interest-bearing loans. For many, higher education is not realistic—whether it be different learning styles, lack of interest, or the expense—and does not justify the end result. Yet choosing to turn one's back on formal education may be frowned upon, discouraging those who opt for that path.

Another conventionally expected career path is one in which the individual chooses a field and sticks with it for years, accumulating seniority and expertise in that one arena—often called "climbing the corporate ladder." It might make logical sense that, by doing this, the individual achieves a long-held goal of consistent achievement over the course of a lifetime.

In at least one of these ways, the people featured in this book had an unlikely start. Some did not complete high school. Some completed high school but had no notion beyond that of what could come next. Some had goals and aspirations, only to be derailed by one force or the other—requiring a change of path. Others exceeded the boundaries of a likely start even more dramatically. Meet the thirteen people in this book, and take a peek into the circuitous roads they've traversed so far . . . from unlikely to unstoppable!

Chapter 1
Why Ted?

Edward F. Collins, aka "Ted" and later, "Doc Lilac," grew up as one of ten children. The family lived on the grounds of the largest public cemetery in Rochester, New York. In his handwritten memoirs, Ted expounded upon the ways that he and his siblings were considered to be odd by their peers as well as the passengers who rode the trolley car—the public transportation traversing the main street in front of their residence. First, he claims the Collins Clan was mocked because they often smelled of manure. His father was hired as assistant superintendent of the cemetery for his skills directing a team of horses. The kids spent many hours in the horse barn playing, occasionally being useful, and oft carrying an unpleasant aroma as testimony to their whereabouts. Second, the ridiculing was linked to their "graveyard" surroundings, perceived by neighbors as spooky, bolstered by "legends of cavorting with spirits, ghosts, and the like."

Unusual to outsiders or not, it was a loving, boisterous family. As is characteristic of many large families, there was a wide age span between the eldest and youngest. The third youngest, Ted was mothered by his older sisters and regarded his two older brothers as heroes. Those relationships endured all their lives and were lovingly chronicled in the diaries of their mother and the progeny who continued her habit of documenting everyday life.

This background matters because, from his early days, Ted was wired to contribute any money that he could to the family. He was motivated to go the extra mile, to put a bit aside to buy some of his favorite things—candy bars and movie tickets as a youth, horticultural specimens and real estate as he matured. From selling newspapers and chickens to hauling bricks, he never shied away from hard work. He prided himself on the constant physicality of what he did, right up until his passing at eighty-nine years of age.

Jennifer Talks Ted

As Ted's daughter, I grew up surrounded by the legendary stories of his hard work. There were tales of scrimping for every nickel, assisting his siblings throughout their lives, as well as many recalling his foibles: being kicked out of high school for punching a teacher, returning after traveling the country to become his class president, enlisting in the army at the precise moment that my mother thought they should be married, working three jobs to get his dream of business ownership off the ground, to name only a few.

Add to this picture a man with a passion for writing and a love for all things outdoors, and the result is a puzzling composite of contradictions. To the child version of me, those contradictions often made our family stand out, regarded as a bit strange. It's pretty well accepted kids like to blend in. Any characteristic of your family that is not like everyone else's can make you feel odd or weird—the idea that being different is unique or interesting just doesn't cross your mind. It sure never crossed my mind until I was in my twenties.

In our blue-collar neighborhood in Rochester, N.Y., every father of every kid I knew worked at Kodak—the film photography giant that once employed over 62,000 people. These dads all worked a predictable 7:00 a.m. to 3:00 p.m. shift, arriving home promptly at 3:30 in the afternoon. On Sundays, the families went to church together, came home, and cooked hot dogs on their charcoal grills.

Not at my house. My dad left before sunrise every morning, long before anyone else arose, to do something I didn't really understand with trees and plants at a fancy country club. It seemed very far away (those fifteen miles *were* worlds away), and he didn't get home until well after bedtime for my brother and me. We had no clue that he left the golf course at 3:00 p.m. and worked at building his own landscape clientele until dark. Best memory from that time? His gravelly voice singing me country songs while my mother warmed up leftover dinner from hours before. I was groggy, but happily awaited his serenade. By the way, I still remember every word to those old country classics, best characterized by "Lovesick Blues."

If that wasn't unusual enough, our Sundays were nothing like anyone else's. The belief in Sunday as a day of rest never occurred to my father. We drove around all day, stopping at homes with rolling, lush lawns mown in orderly rows, accented by rainbows of neatly planted flowers. That entailed sitting still in the faux wood, side-paneled station wagon with my brother and mother while Dad strolled around these beautiful places, clipboard in hand, hoping to attain yet another new customer for his landscape business. As dark settled in, Dad steered us back into the single parking spot in front of our 700-sq.-ft. home, with an even tinier house behind it, the house of the landlady. This lady we needed to speak to politely and dared not let her see us spraying the hose to cool ourselves, because that would increase the water bill. No one else had something called a landlady, at least not one that I could see.

What the seven-year-old me didn't see, didn't get at all, was that this weird, atypical life was not one to lament. It was the life of someone with an entrepreneurial spirit, a man who knew somewhere in his soul that he could not work at Kodak, or Xerox, or any of the other large, local employers. Following in the footsteps of his older siblings, he tried that once. He'd done custodial work at Kodak during the years when he'd been kicked out of high school, a time when he changed jobs almost as often as he changed his clothes. Those experiences taught him there was no way around it: Ted loved the outdoors, loved growing any kind of plant, admired the stately nature of trees with the reverence that many save for heroes. He was driven to do something different. He needed to create an entity all his own in which he could be his own boss, teach others, and be literally knee-deep in making the world a more beautiful place. He was choosing another path.

Sometime in my teens, my perspective changed. I no longer cringed at the fact that he didn't work the regular hours of other fathers. By this time, Ted owned one of the largest residential landscape companies in the region and dabbled in real estate along the way. My eyes were opened to the realization that his work world allowed flexibility, making him available to help when family or friends needed something. When my friends and I needed a truck for a high school parade float, he had one for us. When I wanted evergreens or flowers for prom decorations, my dad found, cut, and arranged them.

The freedom that earlier choices brought to his later years was Ted's gift to our family. A gift much like the trees he loved so much. If Ted's roots were hard work, then flexibility, family time, and quality of life were the results—the leaves, blossoms, and fruit. My mother, brother, my children, and I were all blessed by his innate work ethic and dedication to family.

The other blessing is that Ted had a passion for writing! Along the way, he often wrote limerick-style tributes to those he loved, commemorating special occasions such as birthdays or graduations. In his later years, he wrote memoirs of selected time periods in his life, those that he believed to be most interesting, or perhaps most amusing.

When this project took off, I figured I would use his writings that I'd previously stored in the basement. I thought I knew exactly where they were, just as I was sure I'd already seen the entirety of his recorded musings.

Neither was true. As I looked through the boxes labeled "Dad" or "Save" or "Ted's Stuff," I couldn't find the lined paper with the ragged edges from being torn out of a five-and-dime spiral notebook. I couldn't find his beautiful, script-style handwriting where the extreme pressure of his strong hand had practically embossed the words into the surface below. And, I couldn't find the stapled-together packets with titles such as "Working My Way Across the Country" or "How I Met Janice." Frustrated beyond belief, concerned that perhaps I'd inadvertently thrown out those beloved documents, I found a few unfamiliar, random scribblings and hastily threw them into a small plastic bin.

Those first few scraps held nothing interesting and only added to my dismay. Then, a few pages of lavender printer paper (undoubtedly scrounged from when he'd print off advertisements for his lilac-selling business) captured my interest. What are these? Scanning words not as easily legible as his usual writing, I discovered something he'd written only shortly before his passing. A compilation of lists with titles such as:

- *The Dumbest Things I Ever Did*
- *The Smartest Things I Ever Did*
- *Things I Should Have Done Sooner*

In half-pages of lists, he had captured the essence of his life, of what he considered meaningful. Not what I was searching for, but so much better! Those lists were telling me to get writing, urging me to tell his stories and those of people like him. People who did dumb stuff, but then did smart things, and with a little luck and a lot of hard work, figured out the way to live a life that worked for them.

The last page in the packet was another single word, "Jobs." Twenty-nine lines of various and sundry jobs, described in humorous phrases that told the story of the work portion of his life. Some work was undertaken simply to make ends meet, some to advance his goal of owning a business.

Thankfully, the other writings surfaced several days later, just as I remembered them: interesting passages that he journaled, mostly to keep himself busy and his mind sharp. They have been immensely helpful in adding to remembered information and ensuring authenticity to the vignettes about him shared in this book.

But the lists on the purple pages are the true inspiration, the reason for pulling all of this together to share with others, the wisdom of a man who loved to tell his tales and who is cheering us on from afar as we make sense of the many stories that blessed us all of his nearly ninety years. Stories of hard work, ingenuity, perseverance, and love.

Elizabeth Talks Ted

I met Ted—or Papa—as his most cherished humans called him, while sitting outdoors with Jenny at her home. By the way, it was my first day meeting her as well. Theoretically, sitting down with your new boss could be a nerve-wracking experience, filled with sweaty palms and hopes to impress. But the calm space in which we met, casually, on a sunny patio, adjacent to a property full of rows and rows of grapevines was anything but anxiety producing. It was the start of a new job—but also of a new friendship. As she and I were sharing a snack, sipping wine, discussing syllabi, course design, and teaching philosophies, an older gentleman came zooming up on his golf cart to check in with Jenny on her day, and to inquire about me, the "new girl."

This was Ted. He was loud, commanding, and gave off a "man in charge" vibe. While this was my first impression, I also came to learn that he was sweet, kind, willing to learn, and an excellent teacher himself. You could show him a leaf, talk about a tree or plant, and he would not only know what you were talking about, but then proceed to tell you all about the unique features of your botanical specimen.

He proudly toured me through his nursery, and the view from the golf cart, racing through lilac-scented rows, is something everyone should experience. It was then that I learned that Jenny's Papa built this! This nursery . . . his "Castle on the Hill" if you will, and now, his legacy.

Ted was always learning about the next tree, flower, or quite frankly whatever his family around him was excited about. And, let's be honest . . . that was not always trees. At eighty-five years old, he actually let me teach him how to use an iPad, a device far outside his comfort zone. Ted was also a quintessential storyteller. He always had a story to tell, and not just for the sake of hearing himself talk, but most often to gently share an anecdote, a rare insight, or a much-needed lesson. After spending time with Ted, I realized he was himself a lifelong student. Certainly not via the traditional route, but he pursued knowledge, growth, and new ideas in his own way.

I did not realize how profoundly his success as an entrepreneur was going to impact me until this project came to be. In my early years, I was not entirely confident about what I wanted to do when I grew up. I just knew that I wanted to learn, to which my father replied, "That sounds expensive. . . ." I remember as a young person being asked what I wanted to BE. It was as if by articulating what my future employment would be, then my current self would matter. This conundrum implied that the path before me would become more obvious and validated, and in fact there was AN ANSWER.

So, when my friend and mentor asked about collaborating to write a tribute to her dad by exploring the ideas of "luck," hard work, and success—I could not say yes fast enough! The opportunity to learn, not only from Ted but also from the individuals who were interviewed, helped me further understand that life is not about who you are or what you grew up to be. It's the path you took. What you learned on the journey. The people you met, and the ones you loved and sometimes lost along the way. Maybe, just maybe, the hopes and dreams of an entrepreneur live inside each one of us. And push us to keep learning more.

Chapter 2

Meet the Twelve Other Trailblazers

What do an investment banker, a Vegas disc jockey, a teacher, a property manager, a real estate agent, a salesman, a horticulturist, a hair stylist, a manufacturer of body products, and three contractors from assorted trades have in common? Honestly, starting out, the authors did not *know* if these folks had similar characteristics. We only had an inkling that there was something intriguing about them. The unknown was whether the people interviewed would have anything in common with one another, or with Ted.

As it turns out, they did! In the tradition of qualitative research, the interviews were led by a standard question guide aimed at understanding how the interviewees made sense of their career paths, the ups and downs of carving out a meaningful place in their respective fields, and how they perceived constructs such as failure, luck, challenge, and success. Analysis of these twelve transcripts, as well as of Ted's written memoirs, revealed several common themes. These themes expose ideas about choices and success that differ from widely-held assumptions about how people should proceed after elementary and high school education.

Before we get to the themes, let us introduce each person whose story contributed to this overall understanding of how they moved from unlikely to unstoppable. A brief summary is provided for you to get started, as well as to use as reference as their stories unfold in future chapters.

Jeremy

Jeremy could not get out of high school fast enough. The means to his end was joining the Marines. He grew up in an affluent suburb, where the heads of households were primarily highly educated professionals. His parents were no exception—a university professor and a counselor who expected their sons to choose the same route to success. But Jeremy's ideas were far different. He accelerated his high school education, not to continue on an academic path, but to get out faster and *serve*. He envisioned the military as a place to build his physical strength, help others, and be the best.

He embarked on that path just as he'd planned. An injury during a training exercise brought that dream to an abrupt halt. From butcher to lawn mowing to sales, the next several years were fraught with disappointments and failures aplenty, until he discovered a new, purposeful way to move forward.

Angie

Angie grew up with parents who did not understand her dreams. She had big ones too—maybe an actress? A lawyer? But her mom, one of eleven children, was the only one that graduated high school and suggested to Angie the only paths she knew—a secretary, a waitress, a nurse . . . none of which appealed to Angie. Her father lacked enthusiasm or encouraging words for her, and she felt unsupported and alone on her path to independence. A self-proclaimed C-student, Angie realized becoming a lawyer was "unlikely" to become a reality for her.

In her twenties, after bouncing from one waitressing job to another, Angie met her husband, loved being a stay-at-home mom, and opened her home to care for other children. A mis-step on the stairs and a damaged lumbar spine ended that flow of income and forced Angie to rethink her future. What could this waitress, wanna-be actress pursue now? While she laid up with the injury, she had time on her side to rethink her goals and aspirations. But she needed a quick solution to help support her family. Little did she know that the answer would come to her in a want ad.

Tim

Skateboarding and playing music meant everything to Tim during his high school years. He graduated from a school district that urged everyone to go on to college, so an English degree at the local state university seemed to check the boxes. At least for the moment.

As his college years unfolded, being a disc jockey provided some income, but more importantly, it let him do what he loved—hang out with friends and share a common vibe. His drive for creativity was also nurtured academically, through a creative writing curriculum. But a university career counselor discouraged him by advising: "The only way to achieve any semblance of success with an English degree is to teach English."

Degree in hand, but with no desire whatsoever to teach, music seemed the only way Tim could envision fulfilling his dreams to spend his life being creative.

Laurie

The outdoors, plants, and bugs excited Laurie for as long as she could remember. As a young girl in the seventies, she could not have cared less about any of the careers typically suggested for women. She tried out jobs like retail and food service, but without exception Laurie gravitated toward her love of plants.

It was a struggle to figure out a career path that honored her love of the outdoors. One that came close, a conservation officer, struck her as too solitary. She wanted to be around plants *and* people! She joined a landscaping crew, but found herself in the middle of a sector filled with bias toward women who wanted to perform demanding outdoor work typically associated with men's jobs.

For a few years Laurie found a company that appreciated her contributions, until the company owner, also her mentor, sold the business to someone with such a different outlook that she saw no option but to quit. A young mother at that point, she and her husband encountered one financial roadblock after another while trying to forge ahead.

Chris

Chris's future options were so bleak, he shared at one point that everyone in his family was certain he would end up in jail or dead. His childhood challenges were considerable: constant struggles with school, countless hours alone after school, no father figure, and a mother struggling to make ends meet left Chris to fend for himself far too often. Unprepared for anything else, his entry into the work world consisted of food service gigs at night and jobs requiring extensive physical labor, such as driveway paving or roofing, during the day.

Before long, Chris was a father himself, determined he would do things differently for his child. He just didn't know how, especially when the small business he was working for dissolved. Chris did not have many options, but with a truck and some painting equipment, he resolved to find a way.

Rachel

She knew what she wanted as a middle schooler. Rachel was most happy when styling her friends' hair after school. It was creative and made her friends happy right along with her.

Her high school guidance counselor (whose own mother was a stylist) thought hair styling was a big mistake. His authoritative take on that career, bolstered by his own bias, steered her away from what she loved. She took a couple of college courses, telling herself the college experience was important. Actually, she took one class, the only one that interested her, multiple times. She liked psychology but could not focus, could not pass the course.

Floundering, Rachel took a job or two for income. A wistful conversation with her dad resulted in Rachel finally pursuing the training she'd wished for all along. Certificate in hand, she embarked on a path strewn with the difficulties of starting a career with babies in tow. Many twists and turns later, she was ready to build a business of her own.

John

John wanted to be a stockbroker ever since he was about five or six years old. He and his dad spent time together watching movies, and John was overcome with admiration for Eddie Murphy in the movie *Trading Places*. In that movie, the main character who worked for a Wall Street brokerage firm wore a suit and tie to work daily, carrying his briefcase. As a small child, John walked around the house with his "church outfit" suit and tie, carrying a little briefcase, pretending he was going to work.

As he grew, he carefully observed those around him who were affluent. The lifestyle, the clothes, the homes with elevators—all those flashy displays appealed to John, likely because he did not have any of it. Growing up in a one-bedroom apartment, where he slept on the couch, created in him a drive to become the guys in movies. The problem was, he did not see the path before him. How would he afford the education to achieve this status? Was there a bridge he might take to the "good life"? Could he work his way into a suit and tie?

Alexandra

From the age of six, Alexandra knew what she wanted to be when she grew up: a teacher. She worked hard in school, tutored others who seemed to struggle, and achieved her degree and certification in special education. It was a dream come true! She was able to find a job working with neuro-diverse children and felt she had achieved it all ... until her goals did not align with the administrator's.

Alexandra worked to assist each child to achieve life skills, but sometimes this fell outside the narrow, individu-alized educational plan. This mismatch of vision threatened her continued employment. She quickly realized that her dream, while right in front of her, was fading. How could she reframe her profession? Could she continue teaching in another format or location? Or had her spark for this profession gone out?

Shawn

Shawn claimed to have been an "A" student who was totally bored by school. He had no recollection of any particular aspiration in his earliest years, except that by age eleven or twelve, he wanted to *work*. He found jobs cleaning pools and mowing lawns. Then, during his first year of high school, he just stopped going to school. He wanted the money to buy his own truck and lawn mowers. Shawn would do pretty much anything to accumulate those funds. He confesses that sometimes that meant being on the wrong side of the law.

Eventually, in order to make things right with the legal system and try to qualify for a loan, Shawn went back to school, but not traditional high school. He found a program at the local community college that allowed him to earn high school credits while working. Having accomplished that, Shawn wanted nothing more than to get that bank loan and go out on his own. His parents could not share that vision. They had always worked for large corporations, enjoyed that security, and judged his decisions to be ill-advised.

Shawn jumped from the high school equivalency program straight into a lawn mowing business ownership without one bit of training. He bought out an existing business, recruited his mother to help with bookkeeping briefly, but his vision was too stressful for her. He had no choice but to do it all on his own.

Jessica

The oldest of several children, Jessica was a caretaker for as long as she could remember. Her parents split when she was young, and her mother struggled with mental health and legal issues. Jessica cared for her siblings, perhaps to her own detriment. She aspired to be a teacher, but college posed more problems than she could overcome, particularly as additional family responsibilities fell on her shoulders.

After high school, the best path for Jessica to attain skills and knowledge of her own seemed to be enlisting in the Air Force. There she acquired experience and skills in a number of areas, from administrative work to counseling. Once discharged, circumstances soon found her as a single mother without a proper home for herself and her child. Getting to a place of stability seemed unlikely, if not impossible. That place of near desperation pushed her outside her comfort zone to enter the world of property management.

Paul

Accountant to beverage center owner to landlord back to accountant, now contractor—Paul has had so many goals, so many visions, that it's easy to lose count. Brought up in a middle-class suburb with dreams of carrying a brief-case, Paul struggled through high school, emerging with a fixed idea: the best route to that briefcase was an account-ing degree at the private university nearby, but his grades made that a long shot. Instead, Paul worked a couple of jobs right out of high school, but the limitations became obvious. A degree was calling to him.

Once he had that accounting degree, the briefcase was never enough for Paul. He wanted more and tried to go for every single one of his goals—sometimes several at once. Failure was hard to take, nearly devastating. Nearly, but not quite.

Mona

Mona's dad had a huge influence on how her path started. As an immigrant, he had been tracked by the education system in his native country to be an architect. In accor-dance with that, he pursued that career yet the artistic aspect of architecture did not resonate with him. At heart, he was an engineer.

When Mona started searching for her career options, her dad kept suggesting she consider engineering. She took some time, worked for a mechanical contractor, and off she went into engineering. She was one of three women in her class of seventy-five, and at her engineering company later, one of three female partners in the midst of more than forty men. It was a good career, but several years later, her sister became an influencing factor.

As her own body changed and her sister became ill from cancer, Mona quit the engineering field to embark on producing all-natural body products. A one-woman show, making the lip balm and deodorant in a special kitchen at her home, Mona chose to leave what was familiar and start on a new road.

Unlikely, But Ready to Go

There they are. The unlikely dozen plus one. Each storyteller shared life experiences in a unique way. Unique, but unified by common themes revealed during the interviews and led by their desire to move forward.

The stories are organized into chapters with titles revealing the essence of the themes. After the authors provide theme descriptions, direct quotes from each individual bring their findings to life. The storyteller's own words explain and amplify their personal experiences. Some stories were so rich and detailed that they illustrate more than one theme. In that case, the story appears only once but the astute reader will undoubtedly make connections to other themes along the way.

Each chapter features the storytellers in the same order they were just introduced. Tales of Ted follow the interview results. His memoirs and journal entries provide countless stories and recollections to support the very same themes. Add in memories from those who knew him, and Ted's characteristics align well with the themes prevalent in the interviews. The characters, the portrayals of who and what influenced them, their world views, and the connections made along the way each embody the same tree-like image that Ted's life portrayed. Rather than sunshine and rain, their roots of hard work are nurtured by perseverance and positive attitudes.

Chapter 3

Take the First Step

The first step towards getting somewhere
is to decide that you are not going to stay
where you are.
J. P. Morgan

Taking the first step sounds deceptively simple. There is certainly no shortage of experts or resources directing people where they should go, what they should do, or how to do it. But what if the steps or roads are completely unknown—like opening a map in a foreign country, only to realize you are unfamiliar with its abbreviations and annotations? What if the path is poorly marked or impassable? What if you're taking that first step in uncomfortable shoes that don't fit, cause blisters, and seem suited to someone else? Have you ever felt that the journey is just too daunting, and you haven't even started yet?

Children and young adults are often told they can be anything they choose, and do anything they set out to do. Yet, conversely, philosophers and economists argue about the value of limitless choices. The book, *The Paradox of Choice* (Schwartz, 2004) proposes that more choice can actually be a negative thing; when excessive, too many options are overwhelming and may lead to further indecision.

Some young adults may not believe they have a choice of first steps. They might subscribe to the premise that you are destined for a particular path due to time, circumstance, or even bad luck. What if you were not born into money? What if you were born on the "wrong side" of town? What if disaster kept befalling you, no matter your efforts? Are you simply bound to fail? Or is there always an opportunity to redefine yourself and make your dreams a reality?

Our storytellers represent a whole gamut of preconceived notions about education, station in life, or the role of choice in determining best first steps. What unifies them is that they all DID take first steps. Those steps may not have all been directed toward a particular goal; in fact, in most cases they were not. But they did choose a direction and proceed. They did not allow the lack of a clear path to deter them from making moves.

In fact, one way to conceptualize their journeys is to think about how most of us travel today when in our cars. We program a destination into the GPS and listen to the faceless pilot calculate our every move. Whatever that mystical authority tells us to do, we do it, blindly reacting to the authority of its computerized voice. At times we are so trusting of the GPS that we don't even realize it is taking us off course, to a similarly named yet inaccurate destination, or even on a path that benefits the chain restaurants we pass along the way and not our ultimate goal of the most direct path. Or the most scenic route. We might miss a beautiful sunset glistening on a lake as we obey the computer. Still, GPS does get us there. Like the commonly held wisdom that a straight path from elementary school to high school to college leads to a career, it implies that a definitive path exists, and you should follow it.

In contrast, our storytellers are more like hikers with a compass. After all, in uncharted territories, what good are our phones' GPS apps? Maybe you suddenly realize your phone's charge is only 3 percent. Maybe Wi-Fi is non-existent, or even worse, the cell service bar drops from one to none at the height of your exploration. While technology seems amazing, it can fail. In stark contrast, the weight of a compass, held fast in your hand, provides orientation with the north star, but does not dictate the moves. As one grasps the compass, and the navigator orients themselves, decisions can be made as new vistas appear or as trailside indicators capture one's attention. Steps can be taken at will, and the direction paused or changed entirely without being forced to travel miles ahead to the next available U-turn or major highway.

Regardless of devices or strategies, our interviewees found themselves at a place in time, a physical space or a sequence of events that, for them, pointed in a direction. So, they took the first step and went for it! Could they find happiness on their path? Would they financially support themselves or a family? Were they confident enough to follow their hopes and dreams, or would fear and failure prevail? Only time would tell.

As you encounter each character, you might envision a hand holding that compass, weighing their options, contemplating and ultimately deciding on an individual set of first steps. Some used a structured entity, such as the military, for a way to get ahead until other choices became possible. Others followed early dreams but discarded them for various reasons along the way. And a few found they had to overcome preconceived notions about who could succeed in their chosen field, rise to the challenge, and climb the mountain.

You are invited to follow their paths, no matter how rocky or stormy. You may ponder their choices or cheer them on. Eventually, while discovering what motivated and excited our unlikely individuals to pursue their dreams, you may come to the realization that your first steps await you! Some of these individuals followed early inclinations, making choices that would steer them to today. Some stumbled along or were drawn in other directions before they settled on the path that led them to their current place in life. When it came to an initial choice, in each case, for a whole variety of reasons, only one possibility seemed the viable first step. But would it work?

Jeremy

Jeremy works in the finance industry and by his very nature, holds confidentiality and privacy in high regard. After careful contemplation, he agreed to be interviewed. He'd requested prior knowledge of the types of questions that might be asked before making that decision.

Logging into the virtual interview, it became clear that Jeremy had prepared some thoughts based on the question list. He launched into a well-articulated summary of his early years, describing himself as a teen attending school surrounded by buddies who, like him, were mostly children of professionals. His mother earned a master's degree and created a successful counseling practice; his father's doctoral degree earned him a professor appointment at the local technological university; and he thought of his brother as a genius, "a phenom."

Jeremy considered himself the outlier—a sports guy. He lived to play soccer and wrestle. He didn't really like school for anything but sports and hanging out with friends, had an almost paralyzing test-taking anxiety, and was determined to make as speedy an exit from academics as he possibly could. Despite his parents' success after pursuing academics, he did not see a future in that world. Jeremy wanted to go into the military. And not any branch would suffice—it had to be the Marines, because they were the toughest. In his mind, toughest was best.

The first thing that was obvious when Jeremy logged in was the sparsely decorated office behind him, with wall-mounted televisions broadcasting minute-by-minute details of the current stock market activity. In contrast were the framed photographs of his daughters carefully arranged all around him. He leaned in toward the computer screen to emphatically share, "Probably in eighth grade, I knew I wanted to be in the Marine Corps—that's what I wanted to do, all I ever wanted to do: just something that was very, very hard and something my parents didn't want me to do. I had a fascination with the military and wanted to help solve problems facing the world—I wanted to serve."

Although he knew it would cause his parents angst, he met with a recruiter, spent most of his spare time working out with that guy at the gym, and learned as much as he possibly could about the Marines. As soon as it became legal, at seventeen, Jeremy joined under a deferral program, accelerating his high school agenda, determined to enter the world of his dreams. The recruiter told him of a program that incentivized getting other students to enroll in the program. The previous record for finding others to sign up was three—determined to do better than that record, Jeremy recruited five. This did not go over well with the school principal, as this district prided itself on a high level of college enrollment out of high school. That administrator made it clear to both Jeremy and his parents, through a home visit, that his recruitment efforts should stop.

"Acceleration" and "determination" continued to characterize his time in the military. Number one in boot camp, number one in his class at Camp Pendleton, accelerated in rank to Lance Corporal, in a position to pick any duty station. He was offered "8th & I," which for those of us who don't know, is the oldest active post in the Marine Corps. It supports ceremonial and security missions in the capital, including the Presidential detail. Ultimately, however, Jeremy instead chose to go to Maine as part of the counterterrorism force for the Northeast. In that first meeting, he mused that a tinge of guilt about joining the Marines had made him choose a location closer to his home in the Northeast, to assuage his parents' concern for his whereabouts.

Two years into this elite assignment, during a training exercise, a wrist injury changed everything. "I lost use of my wrist, was medically discharged, honorably discharged, because in the Marine Corps, if you can't hold a rifle a certain way—because all Marines are grunts, riflemen first and then they have a duty second—you can't be a Marine. They said I could go into the Army if I wanted. But that wasn't the best, so no, I didn't do that."

A life plan reluctantly discarded, a self-image changed, but Jeremy had played out his childhood desire to serve in the military. He showed himself, his family, and anyone else that needed to know that he could do it, he could be the best. When it slipped away, he needed to learn how to get back up and make a new plan. Unbeknownst to Jeremy at the time, he would come to rely upon that lesson at least twice more. Life was not done pushing him to change direction.

Angie

Angie's interview started with an enormous smile. Her charismatic energy was so uplifting, it was unimaginable that she actually needed that coffee she was carrying in the late afternoon, doing a delicate balancing act with her huge purse and the equally huge hug she offered as a greeting. She talked a mile a minute, excited and honored to have been asked to share her story. She was almost incredulous that she might have something to offer during the interview, as she had few people believing in her big dreams.

As a kid, being an actress or a lawyer appealed to her. But Angie admitted she had no talent for acting and had "middle of the road" grades, not the ones she'd need for law school. Her dad insinuated that because she was a girl, she was useless, and her mom advised her to select from one of the few work choices she'd been given herself.

"I didn't have that ambition. I didn't even have structure or pushing. It was like 'get out of high school and get a job.' I did my associates degree and thought about going on. I started courses for teaching but stopped and never finished. Too long, too much. I resigned myself to being a waitress, getting a cool apartment, and my life would be set at twenty-two."

Angie put her dreams aside, became a waitress, and eventually moved into an unfulfilling sales position. She met her husband, a master's student aspiring to get an education degree. After they married and had children, Angie stayed home to care for her kids, taking in others' children as well. This plan seemed to be serving Angie well, until a catastrophe struck. While carrying her two-year-old down the stairs, she fell and ruptured two discs, requiring surgery and ultimately forcing her to give up caring for other children in her home. She couldn't lift anything for six months, much less chase children around all day long. While recuperating in bed one day, she came across an ad for a real estate seminar. She and her husband had just bought their first home and she had loved the whole process.

"So I was lying in bed one Sunday after my surgery, and it was like the want ads you know, in the newspaper, and there was a real estate seminar. And I was like, 'I want to go. I think I'd be really good at this.' And my husband was like, 'We're not moving. We just bought a house. We're not moving.' I was like, 'Yeah, but the process was so fun.' So, I decided to go for it. And it was literally like I needed to make a little bit of money because he was teaching, and you know he was supporting us but I was like, 'I just want to get out of the house a little and make a little money. And this seems really fun.' And he was kind of like, 'Oh, how cute. What a great idea.'"

Not entirely supportive, but he gave just enough encouragement to allow Angie to try to return to her own goals and maybe become more than a "useless girl," as her father had previously described her.

Spoiler alert: it worked! Two years later, Angie was making more money than her husband. He was incredulous—he had two bachelor's degrees, a master's degree, a teaching certification, and her income was "blowing up." He ended up quitting his teaching job to join her real estate team. When his mother asked him if Angie was going to be his secretary, you can imagine her surprise upon learning that Angie would be her son's boss! A huge step for them all.

From a "cute" idea to a thriving business. From waiting on others to building her own team. Now with her husband as her employee, he could utilize his skills as the detail-oriented planner, the goal setter, the marketer, all while she helped people through life's challenges to find their homes. Angie had come into her own.

Tim

Skateboarding, hanging with friends, and playing music filled Tim's teen years. He was playing guitar at an early age and then using music to orchestrate his skateboarding sessions. For him, they all went together.

"We all wanted to be pro skateboarders—move to California and live the dream, right? Skateboarding is what got me into music, and then it kind of went from there. But skateboarding for sure. The first idea of hey, I want to do this for real. Thinking about moving away and just going after a passion. Really, really got me going, got me fired up."

Tim started using that passion to DJ during high school events. He met others in the local music industry, which led to nightclub gigs, and gradually they started a series of unique music gatherings he and his collaborators were able to brand as their own.

Yet, growing up in a middle-class suburb, the school district's expectation was for everyone to be college-bound after high school. Accordingly, Tim enrolled at the community college, then moved on to the state university nearby. He aspired to be a creative writing instructor, but his advisor nixed that idea with a strong opposing opinion. "There's no future in writing, son. Smarter to get a degree in literature and teach English." That wasn't going to work for Tim. He needed to be creative.

"I was looking at the whole thing, the details of being a teacher, and I'm like, 'I don't really want to do this.' So, I just started DJ-ing again. And I've never used my English degree for anything."

The party hosting continued in his hometown, until he went to a DJ battle in Las Vegas. Then he *knew*. That scene excited him, gave life to his dream. He knew that staying home, or even continuing the casino circuit a few hours away in Atlantic City, wasn't going to be enough. Family members were hesitant, his father told him they wouldn't see each other much, and people doubted he really wanted to go, but his wife was on board and off they went with only one connection—one person who might be able to help him get set up. He knew it was a long shot, describing the entertainment industry in Vegas as a roller coaster. One connection, an urge to create something, and his wife as a road companion.

Fast forward several years. Tim's interview for this research was conducted by phone as he drove across the desert from one gig to another, his wife once again traveling beside Tim on his journey to solidify his dream to reach larger audiences. Now, he's accustomed to connecting with people and has the confidence to stretch even further, in spite of the competitive, nightlife bureaucracy in a glitzy city thousands of miles from home. He's laid that groundwork, and there is no telling where the road will take him next.

Laurie

Laurie asked to be interviewed in her backyard—an oasis of native plants and wildflowers. We relaxed in the place she has always been most comfortable—outdoors. An apt place for the story to begin, because all Laurie ever knew was what she did *not* want to be, and what she did *not* want to do. Using memories to draw a vivid picture of a little girl squirming at her school desk, she shared her early musings.

"I can't be inside. It was that simple. And it was like that from the beginning, second grade. I remember staring out the windows and thinking, 'I want to be out there, I feel trapped.' Even when I worked at a buffet restaurant, I asked if I could take over caring for the plants—I'd see them hanging there, needing help. I knew I had to be outside, but it took a while to find this (a landscape business). Back then, I didn't know people actually paid for landscaping. I didn't grow up in that kind of neighborhood, where people paid for others to take care of their property."

When she thought of outdoor careers, or spoke with counselors, their suggestions were jobs such as forest rangers, or conservation officers. But she couldn't imagine those for herself either. Laurie is a people lover; those options sounded remote and solitary, not a good fit. Yes, she wanted to be outside but also wanted to be near home, be near people, able to socialize. She'd tried working in a greenhouse and knew she liked both the customer-service aspect as well as the pace of the retail world.

Supportive family members started helping her brainstorm. She recalled a cousin who worked at a local community college, a school that had recently started majors in horticulture and environmental conservation. This cousin described courses like entomology and plant pathology. Her reaction? "That's it—a place where I can study bugs and plants and be outdoors—that's where I've got to be. I loved the classes when we were in the field—out visiting local gardens, even cemeteries had lots of plants to learn about."

Those living laboratories were exciting and affirmed her decision to study horticulture. That was, until it came time to seek employment. She ran into an unpleasant, to say the least, brick wall—being a woman in a dominantly male field in the mid-1970s.

The derisive response she got when calling the vice president of one well-known landscape company about a job? "Honey, unless you're built like a bull, don't bother applying." As she finished imitating the speaker's deep, ridiculing voice, she described the impression it left as "clearly a hierarchy of men over women." It wasn't the first time she'd encountered that mentality, but it felt discouraging nonetheless.

Ironically, the owner of that same company, our own Ted Collins, came to the college a few months later for an interview day. The prior phone call had left her skeptical, but thankfully, her counselor assured her that this guy, the owner of the company, was not of the same ilk as the one she'd spoken to. As Laurie said, "He needed to convince me"—and he did. Ted could not have been more different than the guy on the phone! He suggested she come meet other employees and get a feel for the kind of work they were doing, as well as the whole environment. He ended up hiring Laurie—the only woman in her horticulture class, as well as her good friend—the only classmate of color. If he hadn't sold the business several years later, she says she never would have left. But, he had given her tips over the years for running her own business, by allowing her to run her own division of the company.

Ultimately, Laurie started her own landscape business and garden center. She was able to blend her passion for the outdoors and her love for being around people into a customer-service oriented company, the only woman-owned landscape company in the region. The challenges to come included bankruptcy and too many more examples of male dominance along the way, but she was ready to forge her way.

Chris

Chris, like all the interviewees, was offered the chance to remain anonymous for the interview and book project, but he did not want any of that. In fact, quite the opposite. He arrived for the interview with his operations manager and the first order of business was for her to take photos of Chris and the interviewer to be posted in their social media. He looked upon the interview and the telling of his story as one more way to encourage others like him who struggled through traditional school. After the photos were taken, Chris enthusiastically encouraged the interviewer to ask whatever she wanted; he was ready to share.

Chris finished high school—"barely." When asked what he wanted to be when he grew up, Chris smiled boyishly and said, "You're probably not going to believe it, you'll laugh." He was a kid with a love for dinosaurs and earth science, who aspired to become a paleontologist, and who was dismissed from three high schools in three years.

"I couldn't get out of school fast enough. I was diagnosed with ADHD at an early age. I think that school is one size fits all, but we don't all fit that size. I certainly didn't. Even today, if my job in a company was to sit in an office suite for eight hours a day, I wouldn't be there."

When he did finally make it through high school, he took an array of food service jobs in the evenings, after spending his days as a roofer or waterproofing basements. He was working hard, although struggling to make ends meet when he discovered that he and his girlfriend were unexpectedly going to become parents! He describes that time as a crossroads. Chris realized he did not want his child to have an upbringing like his own—on public assistance, a mother working her hardest to stay out of debt, and a rarely present father.

He recalls thinking, "Hey, look, you need to try to find some kind of steady employment, you have to pay some bills, you have this kid. He can't grow up the way that you grew up—you need to help make it better. So, I ended up having a buddy whose family ran a painting business and needed someone to do snow shoveling for them. I did that all winter, showed I was a hard worker, and they offered me a painting job in the spring. That turned into three years where I learned the trade."

That was good while it lasted. He had a steady income until his employer's family decided they could not all get along and divided the business. He was back to not having a job, had split up with his son's mother, and met another woman he really cared for. Chris had his own truck, a few ladders and tools he'd accumulated, and a person in his life who encouraged him to give painting a try on his own. Chris had spent his young years figuring things out for himself, and he decided it was time to figure out how to run a business. He knew how to paint, but had no clue about the next steps he needed to take.

Rachel

Now in her mid-forties, with more than two decades of experience under her belt, Rachel smiled, recalling that middle school was the time she first thought about hair styling. Tucking her own stylish locks behind her ear, a giggle popped out as she said, "I loved doing my friends' hair and wanted to enroll in the school district's trade program for cosmetology."

That early enthusiasm led her to the guidance counselor's office, to meet with someone she assumed would understand and help steer her in the right direction. What may have seemed a positive thing at the time did not play out as expected.

The counselor's answer was completely negative. "No, you don't want to do that! Your feet are going to be ugly, you'll be all hunched over, and you'll have no life." It turned out the guidance counselor's mother was a hair stylist.

Discouraged by this personal anecdote, she agreed to drop the idea. "As a young girl, I assumed I needed to do exactly what others told me was best. So I said okay and did what I was told. He said I should go to college instead, and I thought the experience would be good for me. I did go, and I really loved psychology. But soon I knew I was going to fail, so I dropped out. I took it again, and stopped again because I could not ever just sit and listen in class. I definitely took it two, maybe even three times, and never passed. What's funny is that now it's a big part of what keeps me interested in doing hair—finding out about people and building relationships—what they do and why."

Rachel floundered for a while and started working at her father's service station, just to earn money. One day, working in her dad's office, she confided in him that she just wanted to do hair. His response? "Well, then just go sign up."

The styling school was behind the station, so she literally stood up, walked over, and signed up for the program that very day. She excelled, felt as if it was the first time she did well in a learning environment. Rachel enjoyed herself, relished the classes that came easily, instead of the struggle she had endured in any school previously.

In her apprenticeship, she was assigned an experienced stylist known for her precision in hair cutting, which served Rachel well. She stayed nearly eight years, until the spouse of the stylist unexpectedly presented her with a business document stipulating a non-compete clause should she decide to leave. She had enjoyed the time learning from her mentor, but the spouse gave her twenty-four hours to sign or leave—basically, an ultimatum. Signing it felt wrong, so she left.

Rachel had a natural talent for hair styling, and she enjoyed her customers. Armed with excellence in her field, a little bit of innate business sense, and eight years of experience, her next choices became how to continue in the field on her own terms. Terms that needed to include surviving a global pandemic, independently supporting herself and her children, and eventually building her own shop and cadre of team members. Rachel was ready to thrive on her own while developing a team happy to be along for the ride.

John

Growing up in a one-bedroom apartment with his parents, John slept on the couch until he was ten. John and his dad loved watching movies; in one of their favorites, John recalls a young actor walking around with a briefcase, working on Wall Street, living the "good life," and he just knew that was the life he wanted. He had friends that grew up on the wealthy side of town, and he recalled being flabbergasted that one four-story house had its own elevator! In his daydreams, he often was the little boy toting a giant briefcase, with numbers swimming around in cloud bubbles over his head.

Financial security was not his only motivation; he described himself as "money driven." However, he quickly learned that not everyone saw his vision. John recounted the story of a friend about to attend a premier university to study technology, who suggested they attend college together. Of course, John's desire was not to study technology, but he thought going to school with his friend was a good plan.

Together they went to the high school guidance counselor. The counselor enthusiastically encouraged the friend. "That university is a good choice. You have good grades." Then he looked John in the eye and said, "But you, John? You do not have the grades for that. I think you should choose a different course in life." Wow, was he taken aback! Subsequently John discovered that not only were his grades a limiting factor in pursuing his briefcase dreams, so was the cost of tuition.

A chance phone call changed all of that. Late one afternoon, John was jolted from a nap by the phone ringing. In his semi-alert state, he fumbled for the corded phone on the couch side table and answered the call that would alter the course of his life! It was a Marine Corps recruiter. He stated he would be at John's high school the next day and wanted to meet with him to discuss a future in the military. Halfheartedly, and rather sleepily, John agreed, fell blissfully back into his nap, and promptly forgot the call. At school the next day, he was called to the principal's office—and begrudgingly made the walk down the long hall, confident they were summoning the wrong person, as he was not the type to get into trouble.

He opened the door to the principal's office and froze in place. His eyes grew wide, and he straightened his posture. *Surprised* would be an understatement, as John was overwhelmed at the sight in front of him: two Marines, fully dressed in uniform, were waiting. Still convinced they had made a mistake, John remained in place, simply curious why these two men were here. While John did not recall the phone call from the previous day, he slowly came to the realization that these men wanted *him*. They believed in him! And despite his grades being "unacceptable" for a direct path to a university, *this* path, with the Marines, was welcoming him with open arms.

John went back to daydreaming of his briefcase and financial freedoms. His next obstacle: John's family did not have the finances nor risk-taking mindset for investing in his future vision. He related that in the book *Rich Dad, Poor Dad* (Kiyosaki, 1997), some families view short term risk as a precursor for long-term investment. His family, however, was more of the poor-dad mindset—where "just getting a job and working there for thirty years until you retire was the safe plan." John had bigger dreams, with visions of dollar signs in his head, and the Marines provided the only viable choice to start him on that path.

Alexandra

Growing up in Puerto Rico, Alexandra had known that she wanted to be a teacher since she was six years old. She giggled a bit recalling this fond memory from that time: "My favorite game was to place all of my stuffed animals on my bed and give them a class."

She eventually attended a university near her home and then moved to Florida in 2017. She joined us virtually online for her interview, from her office in her own micro-school. Bustling children's noises were prevalent in the background, and she frequently glanced off camera with a smile, likely observing "her kids" hard at work in this unique home, converted to a learning environment for neurodiverse children.

"I wanted to be a teacher when I grew up, because my teacher at the time sucked. Back then, they used very old school techniques—teachers were even allowed to hit kids. Teachers, in a position to lead us, were using power to control us, using power the wrong way. At thirteen, I went to an event and fell in love with the idea of being not just a teacher, but a special education teacher. I fell in love with everything—the kids, the parents, the caregivers."

Alexandra compares the various teachers in her life to either "superheroes or villains." When the teachers were able to translate difficult concepts into teachable moments, they were the heroes. But those who saw their role as one of power without compassion, with knowledge but also a demeaning attitude toward the would-be learner, they were the villains. She saw how a teacher could make or break a child, that they had a "delicate power," and it stuck with her. She helped friends who struggled in school, and set up study groups to help classmates by explaining concepts differently.

These early memories and experiences created the foundation of a dream fulfilled—she became a licensed teacher! Her teaching career began in Puerto Rico, and when she moved to the US, she worked at a charter school for children with autism. Her hopes were realized—or so she thought. But she quickly learned that the system to educate children with special needs disillusioned her. She felt the rigid focus on academics left out the other myriad needs each individual child might have.

"I was threatened with losing my teaching certificate because I worked with a child on potty training. I was teaching that child the skill he needed to move on to another school, to be mainstreamed. I was told I was not acting in the best interest of the child, because I was not solely focused on the curriculum and the standardized testing. I got fed up, completely fed up with the system."

During COVID-19, as many educational systems across the globe scrambled for a new plan, Alexandra too had to transition to online teaching. She was incredibly disheartened and discouraged with this format. "I just wanted to be with my kids. Like, I had what I wanted, I was teaching, but not really. And suddenly I didn't know what to do with my life."

She came very close to quitting teaching entirely, giving up on her dream of helping children and their families. Teetering on homelessness and an inability to pay her bills, Alexandra feared losing her dream; it tore her up. Following the rules was going against her gut instinct, her love for children.

But losing her life purpose was not a viable choice.

Then she learned about alternative programs and funding sources. She took a giant leap toward starting her own tutoring center for exceptional children. The state provided the funding, but that was it. There was little guidance, no clear-cut path to recruiting students, and she had her own family to support. Nevertheless, Alexandra was determined to create her own school, her own destiny, and positively impact the lives of the children and families she loved to help. Could this be a sustainable choice? There was only one way to find out, and she took the first step.

Shawn

The authors were familiar with Shawn primarily through his connection to other people. He was known as someone who had made his living in a field requiring hard work and long hours, and as someone who enjoyed his family, his dogs, and his boat (when he wasn't plowing roads in the snowy conditions of upstate New York). We met a character who peppered his stories with lively expletives and enough idiosyncratic expressions to make anyone question whether they were accurately following his meaning. Even starting with a question as seemingly straightforward as describing his role at his business elicited an unexpected response—"babysitting." He affirmed that yes, he considered his role to be babysitter to as many as forty-three employees during the winter.

In an attempt to restart the conversation, we asked Shawn what he thought he would do for a living when he was younger. He shook his head from side to side, then readily admitted that he had no recollection of ever wanting to do anything in particular when he "grew up"; rather, he was "too busy being a kid."

That didn't last long, though. He started working at a pool company at the early age of "ten or eleven?" It seemed to him that he just started to work one day and never stopped. But he did stop caring about school. In spite of being an excellent student, he was bored and thought it was a waste of time. Shawn shared the rather convoluted route he took—in and out of school and legal trouble (or as he labeled it, "the bad side of life"). He dropped out of school to clean more pools and mow lawns, returning to a semblance of organized education only when there was an imperative from the legal system or later, the bank.

"I just left school, pretty much stopped during my freshman year. But I had to go back intermittently to keep my ass out of court. I lived on the wrong side of life for a bit. Bad stuff, but it got me some of the cash I needed.

"When I turned sixteen, I was sure I wasn't going back to school, but I was wrong. I had to go back at nineteen, just not taking the high school route. In order to get enough money to buy a mowing business, I needed a diploma. The community college worked out a plan for me to get a diploma in one semester.

"Oh, and I had to play golf for them in the summer, in order to get a physical education credit. So, after the business class and golf requirement were completed, I walked into the bank and asked for my check. I wanted that mowing business—it seemed cool to mow lawns, cool to have my own truck. The truck was 'boy-fantasy' kind of stuff, for sure."

The bank did loan him some money, with his mother continuing to periodically loan him more—or as he jokingly described it, playing the role of "loan shark" for about five years after that.

Hard work, hard lessons, and daily doses of reality characterized his next few years. Learning about business, learning about employees, and managing competitors all comprised a schooling of real life. Shawn described it as a "backwards progression," three steps forward, two steps back, every single day. The continuous nature of progress, followed by failure, helped Shawn figure it out. "I think for about five, or eight, or maybe even fifteen years, I spent more time fixing things that I could have done right in the first place. I'd think I was doing it right, but then not. Backwards fixing took weeks and weeks. I didn't have the right mentality for it."

Fast forward, and twenty-three years later, the main elements of his business have changed to hardscaping and snowplowing, but the foundation of that mowing business at nineteen sustained it.

Shawn had already been out of school, in the work world for years. He clearly cut those ties and wanted to expand his business. Getting the truck may have been "cool" initially, but over the years those trucks became essential for a business that now seasonally employs over forty people!

Jessica

Not one single thing about Jessica's early years was easy. Her mother struggled with finances and emotional stability. And when those struggles included entanglements with the legal system, the family was too often in crisis. Her mother ultimately hit a low point that put Jessica in the position of needing to advocate on behalf of all the children in the family. Her worst fear in taking any action regarding her mother's neglect was that she and her siblings would be split up. A skinny teenager, barely out of childhood herself, Jessica was forced into a caregiver role for the younger ones. The predicament was heart-rending.

"I couldn't just keep doing what we were doing. I couldn't keep trying to find a way to feed us, making sure we got to school. I couldn't keep being the parent when I was a kid and taking care of the parent."

Jessica told story after story of caretaking for other loved ones and their children, sometimes putting herself in worse economic and social situations just to help out others. Even her father, although he had his own set of difficulties, recognized the burden on her. To this day, she often needs to remind herself the same thing that he said to her, "You can't save the world."

Reflecting on the early days of contemplating what she would do with her life, Jessica considered teaching, specifically desiring a career as a special education teacher. In spite of costs and the childcare responsibilities, Jessica took a few college courses to start down that road but realized she was "too emotional; I just couldn't do it." Her grandfather was retired from the Navy, so a career in the military was something she was familiar with and respected. That beloved and respected man asked her not to go into the Navy, not to follow in his footsteps. Okay, so what did she do? Jessica went into the Air Force.

The Air Force gave Jessica a chance. A chance for the child-woman to tear herself away from the pulls and obligations of family, the opportunity to earn a living while learning skills, and the time to grow up—in all ways. They accepted her into service under the condition that she gain weight. A waiver program allowed her in, but she was separated from others in her class during mealtime to focus on her eating. One more caretaking task—this time taking care of herself.

She left the Air Force behind at the end of her assignment, hoping for better things to come. It was not to be— rather she left the relative security of the service only to face life as a single mother, homeless, living in the office of a mechanical shop, searching for a job, any job.

Desperately seeking employment, knowing she had to earn money, the administrative skills Jessica had obtained in the Air Force helped her see new doors of opportunity. After days of searching through want ads, she told herself she needed to take anything that came along. The next day, a listing for an administrative assistant caught her eye. She took a chance, and a door to the world of property management opened. This, by happenstance, eventually led to an encounter with another staff member. A man she eventually married, who propped up her hopes and ultimately included her in his dream of owning their own business. To this day, she is the ultimate caretaker for extended family in addition to her own, but she and her spouse have built a firm foundation for plotting their future course.

Paul

Paul requested an early Saturday morning interview, hoping to get it done before his wife and kids were ready to start the day. He seated himself in a semi-reclined posture with his legs stretched out in front of him.

Adopting a tongue-in-cheek manner, Paul told the tale of his high school years in a middle-class suburb of Western New York, "I liked it so much, it took a couple extra years to actually get out of there. Then, I went right out and got a job—school was just not for me, or so I thought."

Paul's storytelling style often required us to interpret the meaning behind his colorful words and verbal expressions. His first employer concluded that Paul's skills were wasted in the menial moving job he had chosen, suggesting that Paul had a talent for efficiency and spatial relationships that were atypical of most guys doing the same job. "That guy, the boss at that first job, fired me. When he checked what I'd done that first day, he said I packed the moving van so square, so efficiently, that I had to get out of the moving business and go to school. Maybe I would have eventually figured that out myself, but not that quickly."

Following the advice of that perceptive man to go back to school, Paul took the community college route before applying to an accounting program at the local private college. Why that route? He confessed that his school grades had not been up to the college requirements.

Why accounting? Much like John, his motivation was a briefcase! "I used to walk around in high school with a briefcase. Everyone made fun of me and that briefcase. But I always knew I liked business. My friends' fathers were accountants. I'd talk to them and ask questions. I figured out that if you're going to do anything, you need a life plan. And to achieve that life plan, I needed this degree in order to secure that income. To get that income, I needed this kind of job. Was that great? No, but I got through it. What matters is the first job. After that, experience kicks in."

Paul described his innate nature as "an a.m.-er"—a morning guy who liked to get up early and do things, get going. Many times during our conversation, he spoke of how his body would tell him what he could and couldn't do, what his activity level should or shouldn't be.

Pointing to the place on his wrist where a watch might be, he declared, "I've been an a.m.-er my whole life. Doesn't matter what day it is, no matter what time I go to bed. At twelve years old, I wanted a paper route. So, I got up at five a.m. on Sundays and stuffed papers. Grabbed a cart and around the neighborhood I went. In the winter, I'd wake up my mother, tell her I needed a ride, and gave her some money to drag me around. From an early age, I wanted to be a doer, an entrepreneur."

We found ourselves talking to a guy who had studied numbers, wanted to be active, admired entrepreneurs, and had a certain income in his mind from day one. Oh, and when he got out of college, in addition to being an accountant, he thought he wanted to be in real estate. And, buy a business! It was tiring just listening to all that he wanted to do, wanted to accomplish. At one point or another, he was determined to fit it all in. But the accounting degree? That was his safety net. Paul lost count of the times he'd try something entrepreneurial—one of his many goals—then return, as he put it "to corporate America," back to the steady income. Being an accountant had regular hours and a predictable income that suited his growing family's needs. But it didn't fuel his fire, and it didn't satisfy his need to build something that he could someday show his kids, to create a legacy.

Obtaining the accounting degree, then getting the adult briefcase, became the vehicle that drove him toward his other goals. With each business failure, his return to "corporate" steadied him enough to recalibrate and step into the next venture with more experience and maturity under his belt. The years brought plenty of hardships—including bankruptcy and divorce. Ultimately, he achieved self-proclaimed entrepreneurial success by being a contractor in building and construction. But he sees more steps to come—he wants to shift his role. In his words, it's time to "stop doing and start overseeing."

Mona

One of our other interviewees suggested Mona might be an interesting person to consider for this project. The story of her beginning to develop natural body products after her sister's cancer diagnosis was not only emotionally captivating, it seemed to have the potential to highlight a very different path from any of the others.

Finding a time to meet was not easy, as Mona's business is primarily a one-woman show, she was an engaged community member, held another part-time job "just for fun," and is a devoted mother. Granted, her children are in their early twenties, but when the interview was scheduled, one had a medical issue demanding her time as well. On the appointed day, only a couple of minutes into the interview, the story became even more compelling: mid-career, she had walked away from her life as an engineer to embark upon an adventure in a completely different direction.

"Mona Moon Naturals was never a business I planned on creating. When my sister was diagnosed with breast cancer in 2015, it was all very eye opening to me."

It seemed like her career was set early on. After high school, Mona initially studied architecture, moved into civil engineering, and established herself in a company she liked. By the time she was in her forties, the only thing holding her back was a total inability to pass the professional engineering examination.

"In the engineering world, your course in life is that you get your professional engineer's license. I did not. No matter how many tests I took, how many, I couldn't do it. I would go to classes at night. No matter how many refreshers, nothing. I couldn't pass the test to save my life. I wasn't a partner at the time, and that lack of a professional engineer's license was a big hurdle in the minds of a number of the partners. Then I had this great opportunity to start working with one of the partners who was doing business development. And I was very successful. I made the business a lot of money, the company a lot of money. And, I stuck with it."

Ultimately, a change of the guard at the company and an expanded role in business development allowed her to remain in that position despite lacking the coveted credential. Mona advanced, supported herself and her children, and expected she would retire from that position.

But when her younger sister was diagnosed with breast cancer, Mona not only stood by her sister every step of the way, she also walked away from that successful career, and toward a new path. She learned more and more about harmful chemicals in deodorants and cosmetics, vowed to do things differently, and tackled the problem head-on. As an engineer, she'd learned to be a problem-solver.

"I wouldn't trade my education for anything in the world. It teaches you how to be creative and solve problems, which you need for anything you do in life. So, I had a problem. Deodorants already on the market were too harsh or didn't work, so I figured out how to make it myself. It's like figure it out—reverse engineer things."

Those skills and her strong beliefs catapulted her forward to a whole new set of goals. She's yet to make a substantial income from it, is trying to determine how to effectively share the load she's carrying on her own, but is determined to keep going!

Ted

Born at home in 1928, Ted's early stories took place in a house provided to his father, a benefit that came with being the assistant superintendent of a large city cemetery. They were not easy times—he was born during the depression—but his father's job and the many acres available to raise vegetables helped them through. His journals depict it well, starting with the claim that he thought he must have been born at about six years old because he cannot remember anything sooner.

"I do remember having to repeat fourth grade at #42 public school, and a kind teacher convincing me I would be better off because of it, comforting me with assurances that I had real possibilities. I may have been afflicted with some degree of ADD (attention deficit disorder) then, but her encouragement (or, in his words, "prescription") worked, and I'm thankful for her interest and wisdom. I settled down, excelled in cursive writing, and to this day, read a lot and do 'rithmetic without calculators. So, life began, it seems at eight or nine, thanks to caring parents in drastic times. I was skinny, plagued with earaches, toothaches. That said, I was very energetic, often tireless."

Ted worked at almost anything to earn money—some jobs may even seem comical in retrospect. These various, mostly menial, jobs were interspersed over the years through times when he was in school, times when he was expelled (for punching a teacher), a year and a half of working at farms and parks while he and a friend made their way across the country on an adventure in the 1940s, before and after being in the military, and finally when he settled on a vocation.

Ted left his daughter and grandson with strong evidence about the choices made, the ones regretted, and the ones he regarded as the best. Sometime in his late eighties, he penned informative lists that were only found within the last year. The choices he named as his "Smartest":

- Marry Janice
- Return to high school and attend college
- Business of my own
- Work at Oak Hill Country Club with its exposure to 800-some potential customers
- Following Janice's hunch to purchase a home on Turk Hill Rd.

These are notable for what they say as well as what they leave out. His love and admiration for his wife,

Janice, is evident and endearing, something to be cherished. Numbers 2, 3, and 4 lack details, making his work path sound deceptively simple. In reality, those steps were anything but simple.

Ted needed to beg his way back into high school, with his father assuring the principal of good behavior going forward. Once back in the classrooms, he excelled. He was too old to play high school sports but instead helped coach baseball and basketball, was elected as student body president, and his academics were outstanding for the first time in his life. Within a couple of months of returning to high school, his younger sister introduced him to one of her classmates, Janice. He aspired to either politics, journalism, or horticulture and looked ahead to his future with the love of his life. They were engaged within a couple of months of high school graduation. But his deep sense of patriotic duty drew him to enlist, and he qualified for the Army Security Agency with assignments in Arlington, Japan, and Korea.

After three years of service, the G.I. Bill facilitated enrollment in a two-year, degreed horticulture program, solidifying the choice between Ted's three aspirations. He and Janice picked up and left shortly after their wedding to start his much-delayed schooling. Returning home from college with his expectant wife, work was again a necessity. They moved in with his parents until he could save enough money for an affordable residence. As he tried to build a fledgling business, he was both blessed with good connections from his gardener's role at a beautiful lakeside estate, and cursed with the realities of earning enough to sustain a business and his family.

"Along with business growth, however, came growing pains and financial problems. I was told by a friendly banker that the seasonality of the landscape industry was preventing me from getting necessary loans and suggested a full-time job for a couple of years and letting others in my employ actually run the day-to-day."

Although it was a stop along the route that he had not anticipated, that banker's urging led to his employment at a prominent country club. The club was actively seeking an expert arborist. His work there became highly respected by the Board President and members, leading to a good relationship with many potential future customers. In fact, one of Ted's most often told and retold stories, interspersed with his own laughter, went something like the following.

"One day close to the time I was ready to turn in my resignation and get back to my own business full-time, I went in to greet the ladies who worked in the office, bringing them donuts as I often did. One was working very busily and barely looked up from alternating between her Rolodex card file and her keyboard. When I asked her what she was doing, she told me they were converting their list of members to the computer and didn't need the Rolodex any longer. I asked her if I could have the cards she was tossing in the garbage, and she gave them to me! That became my first customer mailing list."

Ted struggled with the seasonal nature of the landscape business he loved and its financial challenges for many years before growing to the point of selling that profitable company and evolving into a new role: a life of managing his commercial real estate while pursuing his passion for growing and selling lilacs—the official flower of his hometown. Throughout it all, he drew upon his deeply ingrained work ethic, his ability to talk to people, and his good humor to spur him forward until his final days.

A few more thoughts ...

Lao Tzu, an ancient Chinese philosopher, is credited with saying, "A journey of a thousand miles begins with a single step." When our interviewees took their first steps, some had a clear direction of where they intended to go, others were compelled to do *something*, make any kind of forward motion, no matter where it might lead. None knew if there were a thousand miles ahead or an immeasurable trip. Whether they would get there or not is yet to be told. There was no way to anticipate the challenges to come. Challenges from people singling them out, telling them they didn't belong, or would never make it. Obstacles arose in the environments around them that affected the whole country, even the world. Regardless of the source of the potential bumps in the road or detours, something kept them going, kept them taking single steps—not always forward, but moving, surviving, slowly carving the paths that inform these stories.

Chapter 4

Navigating
the Hard Road

*Nothing in the world is worth having or
doing unless it means effort, pain, difficulty. . . . I have never in my life envied a
human being who led an easy life.*
Theodore Roosevelt

Many people endlessly seek the easy, smooth path to
follow. Yet literature, poetry, biographies, even motivational speakers address the phenomenon of taking
a challenging path or finding one's way even after being
discouraged by trusted family and friends. There is Robert
Frost's classic poem, "The Road Not Taken" which heralds
the difference made in one's life by taking the less-traveled
fork in the road. Or, in the similarly titled, ground-breaking
best-seller, *The Road Less Traveled* (Peck, 1978), the author
suggested a framework for living with the premise that life
is hard, challenging for even the strongest among us. Dr.
Peck leads the reader to accept, and ultimately transcend,
those challenges.

The drive to seek the easy road is not by any means unique to travel. Just scroll any social media account you have, and it is a nonstop barrage of vacation photos, people "living their best life," using hashtags like YOLO (you only live once) and FOMO (fear of missing out), all the while posting just a single, nearly perfect, moment in time. If you are not careful and misinterpret these images and ideas as that person's everyday life, you can quickly be disillusioned by it all. Tricked into believing that everyone has it easy, that becoming a YouTuber, or an Insta-famous influencer is the only way to go.

"Easy money" or making a "quick buck" can be glamorized, even chased. Stories abound regarding people who were scammed by sales pitches or pyramid schemes, all in search of wealth without effort. The news carries stories almost every day about people making thousands per week on a "side hustle." As appealing as the easy road may appear, a little investigation reveals that true instances of making it to "easy street" are few and far between. Many of our interviewees were openly vocal about taking the hard way to do things, or that being told no only served to make them more determined, even re-energized, to move forward. While obeying no or acquiescing to the naysayers may have been easier, or less painful, the individuals we spoke with emphasized that "easy" didn't enter into their experiences along the way.

Jeremy

The medical discharge from the Marines was devastating for Jeremy. At loose ends, life plan derailed, he was not ready to go home yet. He stayed in Maine and found a job as a butcher. One day, he made his way to the soccer field at the University of Maine and was happily blowing off a little steam, dribbling the ball around after work. A man approached and asked him if he was planning to play for the school. Discovering that Jeremy had no connection to the school whatsoever, he surprised Jeremy with quite the offer—the man was the university soccer coach!

"You know, I'd like to have you try out for the team, become part of the team, but you'd have to enroll in the school."

Jeremy's love for soccer had never faded. Thinking he certainly had nothing better to do, he decided maybe this time he could go to school, go for the chance to play soccer. He enrolled and chose the only open course left for the semester. It was advanced technical writing. Some might say that playing soccer for the University of Maine would be the natural way (the easy way?) to get an education and figure out what to do with a completely upended life plan. How difficult could that be? Take a few classes to play the sport he'd enjoyed as long as he could remember. But sitting in that classroom was not the answer for Jeremy.

"For someone that just got out of the Marines, always hated school, it was the worst course you could ever possibly take. I played my first game, had a great game. Went to my first class, hated every part of it, and decided that it was just not right for me."

That sealed it—he left: left Maine and went back home, to his parents' house, arriving at eleven o'clock at night. In his mind, maybe he could now make it up to his mother—make up for enlisting and moving far away. He slept in late that first morning, languishing a bit in his old room, enjoying the feeling of being back home. When he finally got up,

Jeremy was greeted with the realization that this home-coming was not going to be easy.

Seemingly still astonished to this very day at what he found awaiting him, Jeremy relates, "A note on the kitchen table, a note on the table from my father. My father, the overachiever. It just said, 'Get a job.' I'm pretty down on myself at that point. I'm a dumb Marine with no skills—if I can't fight and protect, what skills do I have? Can't make money playing soccer."

Complying with his father's demand to get a job right then and there was anything but simple. He was too discouraged with the way his dream had ended. Down on himself, absorbed by what he was unable to do, he could not fathom finding a job. And that night when his father realized no progress on the employment front had occurred? He told Jeremy that if he couldn't find a job, he needed to "make a job." When Jeremy protested that he didn't know what that even meant, his father did not back down.

"You're an able-bodied person, go find a lawnmower and mow a lawn."

Jeremy was not going to face another evening of admonishment. He did actually find a mower by the side of the road. He recruited his elementary school librarian as his first customer, and almost before he knew it, her neighbors signed on as well. Then he cut hedges, then he plowed driveways and parking lots. A few years later, he had accumulated eight employees and three trucks. He also had a wife, an infant daughter, and very little money.

"I decided I needed to do one of two things. Either find a way to grow the business exponentially or sell it. I ended up selling it. And I was looking at a debt of $100,000 for five years."

Unlikely to Unstoppable

Jeremy found himself, yet again, in need of a job. This time, not at his father's urging but because he needed to do something to feed his young family. Maybe staying the course to grow the business would have been easier, maybe not. Opportunity came along with his decision to answer a want ad for a sales position, but so did challenges.

Without even knowing what the company at the other end of that phone call sold, Jeremy just heard that they were willing to hire and train him. Hiring and training sounded better than nothing, so he chose a path strewn with unknowns.

Tim

Las Vegas definitely offered a bigger market for Tim's disc jockey skills. It required a move across the country and starting over. In his hometown, he'd developed a good reputation and established a following. He and a friend coined a brand name for their social events. It had garnered attention and become a thriving business model. Going to a new place, a bigger city, held promise but there were no guarantees. In fact, maybe the idea that was noteworthy in a small town would be silly or passé in a more cosmo-politan location. He characterized the new environment as a roller coaster, where the bottom could fall out at any minute, and he had to make his own way.

"Hearing the word no when I asked for a booking or being told, 'uh, that's not the best look for you' was a big challenge at first. There were established insiders, and I wasn't one of them."

Tim describes a competitive environment with most DJs involved in an intricate arrangement, consisting of both direct contracts with the entertainment venues and some agency work. It required patience and self-reflection to navigate being the outsider. He also found he had to take criticism and find an alternative way of looking at it.

"I think when you get those darts thrown at you, or you get criticism, it's all about how do you deal with that. Does it motivate you or drive you down? For a long time, I was kind of scared of criticism, but now I more or less see it as a challenge, or a chance to refine a tool. It's already pretty sharp, right? I kind of want to know what they think, I want to know if you care about it. Or, if you don't, why don't you? I'll push forward from there."

His affinity for the creative side to his business also kept him going whenever a hard *no* came his way. "What helped me sustain myself through that would probably be the creative outlet, the party, the spirit. I think as long as I had this vehicle, I know I'm not dead in the water. As long as I have something that I can go and create and pitch to somebody somewhere, they could possibly like it. I'll be okay. The challenges don't go away, there's new ones every day."

Tim realized there were a lot of people vying for the same work. But, in the end, the agents or entertainment gurus have to like your product. He learned eventually to establish a base, be confident in what he had to offer, and to do what he does well. He also reminds newcomers to the field that even what seems like a small gig can turn into a bigger opportunity.

"I want to work harder, because I want those people that are here to talk about it. To tell somebody else it was good. So, I gotta be super good, because I'm creating a word of mouth. Don't take any gig for granted. If you agree to do it, you gotta go full charge."

Going "full on" is what helped Tim face being turned down, convert criticism into an opportunity to do things better, and grow a new brand in a new town. After years of improvising, he now has more structure to his work life. Not only is he working very steadily himself, he has started a limited liability company and is able to subcontract other, newer disc jockeys and place them in venues.

Laurie

It's already been made clear that Laurie's preferences would not allow her to take the easy way. She saw no future for herself anywhere but in horticulture, landscaping, or ento-mology—the choice to be in these fields as a woman in the 1970s was destined to be an uphill climb. It was a climb from which she would not retreat.

When she first visited the landscape company at the behest of the owner trying to recruit her, she was wearing, as she describes it, "a cute little outfit." Her new employer recognized the challenge such apparel would bring her in the environment: "This will be the last time you wear something cute like that. We got a lot of guys around here, and the next time you come, it's gonna be a t-shirt and jeans."

Somehow, Laurie knew right then and there that he wanted her to succeed. Ted became her mentor, her champion. In a few short years, she was running one segment of the business, the lawn care/pest management portion. She was involved in all aspects of running that department—marketing, learning to budget, recruiting new customers, and managing its salespeople (actually, sales*men*).

The owner and his finance manager set target goals for sales, and she exceeded every one of them. They had incentivized the periodic totals for each department and those who met their target. "I hit them every single time, because I wanted to go to St. Thomas!"

That owner who had brought her in eventually sold the business. The new guy? He had a very different plan for employee payment. No more commissions, no more incentives. Only a base salary, and a toxic culture to boot. Before she knew it, this turnover in ownership presented unwelcome challenges for Laurie. She had to make a change in her plans, a change that set her on her way to business ownership.

"I just remember that new guy screaming at me. One day his face turned red and I was sure he was having a heart attack. I couldn't stay any longer in that kind of environment. I had a baby, and even though I was making more money than my husband at the time, he supported me in that decision and I left."

Another example of the hard way for Laurie? Fast forward a few years to when she decided to buy a huge piece of property, which included a garden center. At the time, Laurie didn't know much about selling plants in the retail market but figured it would help grow the landscape business.

What she didn't count on was the real estate closing on the property occurring far later than projected. Due to delays by attorneys and banks, she had lost income for April, May, and June. And July was the worst time of year for a garden center: too hot and dry for anyone to purchase plant material in Upstate New York. The huge overhead of the building, with no customer sales to sustain it, set her back to the point of not knowing if she would be able to make payroll. So she and her husband sold their four thousand square foot home and moved into a trailer to cut back on expenses. Asked to reflect on what it took to make those transitions, to make it in her own business in this field, Laurie is unequivocal.

"Commitment—not only commitment, but I'd also say being stubborn. People told me, when I was trying to make a business of primarily lawn pest control, that I wasn't going to be able to make it. I was told that I'll lose customers. But I'm like, 'Don't tell me what I can't do.' So, I did it. And that's what I've continued to do. Trying to be a pioneer. If I read something new and interesting in the industry, I'm thinking 'let's try that here.'"

A committed, stubborn, pioneer woman who set out to prove her critics wrong. A smart woman traversing a man's world—loving plants, insects, and dirt beneath her fingernails. She even won an award for excellence in responsible pest management from a leading university. Laurie's business is thriving. There are several divisions, including pest management, a huge garden store characterized by native plants, and an event venue in the large renovated barn. Events and classes are offered throughout the year including do-it-yourself seminars related to gardening, local music, and seasonal celebrations. She found her niche in a male-dominated field and surpassed everyone's expectations.

Chris

Chris jumped into painting on his own very much on the fly. He was content working for his friend's family business one day, then had no job the next day. Part way through telling this story of starting out on his own to try to support his young family, Chris reflected on the way he grew up as an explanation for how he ventured forward. While he lamented the many hours that he spent alone as his mother worked extra hours struggling to make ends meet, or all the times he acted like the goofball trying to make his class-mates laugh rather than do schoolwork, he also proposed an upside to those difficult years.

"That's the story of my life, I've always had to try to figure it out, being the knucklehead. When someone says, 'Hey, you can't do this,' I'm gonna try. I'm gonna see if we can do it. I don't quit on things. I try to exhaust every opportu-nity, every angle, look at it from every different way. It's the way I grew up. I mean, I had to learn to fight for myself and figure it out. It's to my benefit now. I'm a big believer that if you've been through things like that, traumatic events and a rough upbringing, and had to come up against the odds, I think it actually sets you up for more success. I think it's harder to come up from no adversity than to be taught (later) how to fight for things."

At one point, he remembered his mother telling him that although there was no official diagnosis to support it, she was sure he had oppositional defiant disorder. The very definition suggests that the person refuses to follow others' requests, although interestingly, the characteris-tics are also similar to a child who is strong-willed. She questioned, with not just a little frustration, why he always had to do things his own way. And his wife, whom Chris credits with being his biggest supporter, once put it to him another way.

"There's something missing with you—a little bit to the point where you're able to continue to just freakin' go. When a lot of people would veer right, you're gonna keep going left, or they're going this way, but you're able to kind of go that way."

She's amazed that it somehow works out. Chris initially describes his attitude as "kind of stupid," then corrects himself and suggests that it's more like "blind faith" and an assuredness. He said he's come to think of it as being calm in the face of adversity, when everyone else thinks the "sky is falling." He even speculated that if the sky truly was falling, he'd still assume the same demeanor to assist those around him. Staying calm and self-regulating served him as an eight-year-old and serves him today as a man.

Rachel

Tough times often come about when more than one challenge pops up at the same time. Much of the hard road for Rachel came about due to events in her work life coming at times when her personal life was also stressful.

She was a stylist in the shop of a former classmate for several years. The shop owner and her husband invested with Rachel in another location. Business was rolling along, the working relationship was beneficial for all. It was a good arrangement and Rachel felt she was on the right path.

Soon after, her marriage fell apart. In the middle of the next quarterly meeting at a favorite restaurant, the couple said they had big news. Rachel remembers that it was April Fool's Day, so she wasn't too sure about what was coming next. Next thing she knew, they were asking her to sign a nondisclosure agreement before they spoke any further. In the past, with different people and a different document, Rachel had once been asked to sign a non-compete agreement, and this new request made her wary.

"I said to them, 'I'm not signing a nondisclosure. First, we're out to dinner, second, I've known you for ten years. I'm not signing this without being advised.' Then they came out with, 'We're selling everything.' First, I thought it was a joke, then I just excused myself and escaped to the restroom."

In that restroom, the past several years and all that had happened swirled around in her head. She thought about her two babies, her recent split, not knowing how she would have the money to do anything, no less to buy them out. The proposal that they didn't want her to disclose to anyone entailed her buying out the salon she managed so they could retire and go south. But if she didn't agree, were they expecting her to just drop her clientele and get a position elsewhere?

"I told myself that I hadn't yet put any money in and they were giving me an opportunity. After that meeting, I drove straight to my parents' house, saying what am I going to do? They weren't telling me to go for it, take it. My dad knew too well what it takes to run a business. I'd had a lot of changes in my life, and I think they were pretty hesitant. So—I got a loan on my own. Got it from SBA (Small Business Authority). I actually brought my dad to the accountant so the accountant could tell him I could afford it. He wasn't really convinced, but I paid it off within a couple of years."

Not the road she expected. Not an easy road, but the single mom of two young children figured it out.

John

Having decided at an early age that the "briefcase" life in his "church suit and tie" was the ultimate goal, John had a long road ahead of him in order to achieve that success. He describes being motivated at a young age to make money. "I was money driven—because I didn't have any. I saw people that did. I saw the kind of lifestyle they had and how they lived. So, I always wanted to, you know, kind of emulate that. That was why an office job was not for me, because in sales, if you work harder, you can earn more. So that was always a big driver for me."

One example of how he was going to make money, stemmed from a trip to Miami. "I wanted to rent a car, and I went with my friend and got a Porsche, because I wanted to be driving this Porsche! So, I was asking the guy who owned the dealership, how do you get in this business? You know, what would you do with this and that and he kind of talked to me a little bit about it. And so then I said, 'You know what, I want to own a luxury automobile rental business!' Now, at the time I didn't have any money, but I had the ideas and I had an 'okay, so let's do this' mindset. And so I spent weeks and weeks and weeks preparing a business plan and putting it together. My bachelor's degree was in business, so I was trained to make a thorough business plan. Then I went and found lenders to fund my deal, but the problem was I needed to have my own money. They wanted me to have skin in the game. I was looking for $2,000,000 for a startup, and I needed to have at least twenty percent. I didn't have twenty percent."

So while that big idea did not come to fruition, John stayed the course on the hard road. He knew he had great ideas and the ability with his finance background to put the plans into place, but he just was not yet at the right place at the right time. John saw that his family perceived work as an end unto itself, in contrast to the others he wished to resemble. He once again described the premise of one of his favorite books to illustrate how his views differed from those of his family.

"That book? *Rich Dad, Poor Dad*? It's about how this gentleman, the author, had a poor father whose mindset was to work, go to work every day for the same company and work for 30 years and retire. But the rich dad: his mindset was to own businesses, own assets that made money, and that way he could do whatever he wanted. And, you know, retire early. So I always wanted to trade up. I wanted to transition to that mindset of building businesses and having assets that make you money. I remember being in college and going to buy a house and my parents talked me out of it. They were afraid of the risk. And I wish they hadn't. Because if I had taken that risk, I would have propelled my success a lot sooner."

That disappointment stuck with John and fueled his desire of moving forward to take risks. He talked about a specific time in this transition, returning from the military, and enrolling in a local university. "My friends from high school, I knew that they weren't good role models. Most of them ended up in jail or ended up just not doing anything. So in college I surrounded myself with individuals that had the same mindset as me, and they were able to help me. I used those relationships to propel my success. And I networked with like-minded people, and then we would meet people and get together and brainstorm ideas. We started businesses, we started a hookah business in college, an online electronic business. It's been a nice, long journey."

But certainly not an easy one. No one provided him the path; he paved his own way. Determined at every turn to find success and financial freedom, despite the risk and unknown outcomes.

It was this mindset that propelled John into the future. "I was always going against the grain, going down the road that's less traveled, just always thinking outside the box and willing to take risks. You know, millionaires take more risks. You have to be willing to start, even if you might fail. And so it's just that mindset, that positive mindset, not thinking of what could happen if I fail, but thinking of what's gonna happen when I succeed." And succeed he did. That little boy, who dreamt of a briefcase and a successful life, now supports his family, trades stocks, and continues to push himself down the road less traveled.

Shawn

Approaching Shawn's expansive headquarters, one might never suspect that he spent decades traveling the hard roads. The refurbished barns adjacent to his residence are his sanctuary, from which he controls a buzzing enterprise. On this beautiful, rolling acreage in a rural area, he has created a massive, modern space. Adjacent to his high-tech office area are rows of trucks and snowplows in garage facilities. Shawn sits behind a sprawling desk with several enormous television screens from which he can monitor dozens of cameras mounted around the county to keep watch on the commercial lots plowed by his crew.

When asked to identify three words to describe his path so far, Shawn focused on one word—*irregular*. Not only is it irregular, but laughing at himself, he noted that he had chosen "irregular" time after time, situation after situation. Shawn's tone was reflective, tinged with solemn realizations about the implications of his past decision-making.

"Yeah, irregular, every day. I think your struggles are your own, but in reality, they're probably the same as fifty other people.... It's just a matter of a different address, different weather, different temperature, different choices. My path is very familiar to me. Imagine you have two or three different ways around a golf course—one's flat, one's more like a mountain. I'm on the same golf course as the fifty other people in my business or lifestyle, but it's just a matter of which paths you take to get around that course. Some go up and over it, some go around it, or go through the middle and find the path of least resistance, right? So for me, my way would always be the hard way, at least for quite a bit of my life."

Continuing on, he suggested that sometimes the irregular nature is one that he knowingly embarked upon himself; other times, it was the circumstances around him that led to the hard road. Shawn shared more than one example of feeling like an outsider when he first started his own business. He began with lawn mowing only, expanded into snowplowing and hardscaping, but acceptance from others in similar businesses did not come easily. In fact, he felt rejected by them and their total lack of anything resembling collegiality. He recalls one man who had been in the business for decades. Shawn was working hard to develop a name, to brand his business and be recognizable. This older man made a remark that stung, although Shawn now admits it served as motivation for years to come.

Those stinging words? "Hey, punk, you're a loser. You don't belong in this business." Shawn was promoting his business for the first time at a local garden show. The man with decades of experience sat down next to him to shake his hand, but then shot him down. Shawn thought maybe it was his own nonconformity (confessing he'd never done well with rules). He came into the business at a time when the long-established local industry groups were trying to respond to new strategies for marketing, namely, social media. Those experienced folks were practically hand-wringing over the impact of this new approach on their prior advertising strategies. Shawn didn't have the patience for hesitating or grousing about it. He couldn't see himself at those round table meetings with his competitors. Rather, he simply jumped in and began to use social media to his advantage while it took time for the others to catch up. And it worked for him. Ultimately, his approach convinced others as well.

"Eventually, that same guy used to call me almost every morning. We became friends. We talked for years; I had great conversations with him. It was never about how that guy was doing; he was interested in me. He never knew it, but him calling me a 'punk that didn't belong' became a driving force. That, to me, was my motivation. People telling me I don't belong—I wanted to create something to show them. I was told no, told I couldn't—it inspired me."

Shawn developed an unmistakable brand. He aggressively marketed and chose a bright, flashy color that no one else in landscaping or snow plowing was using. And, everything was that color—a whole fleet of mauve trucks, shirts, folding chairs, seat cushions, recyclable shopping bags. He didn't do things the way everyone else was doing them, still doesn't.

Twenty years later, Shawn summed it up: "I would never change the way I do my business or do my day based on someone else's words. But there are certain people's words that make you think." Stinging words, but they served as his motivation for years.

Jessica

The world of property management was entirely new to Jessica. She had experience in basic administrative functions, but the environment required skills and knowledge beyond those. Still juggling childcare with trying to learn the ropes, she met her future husband—he was a maintenance man for the same company.

A couple of assignment changes later, Jessica and her husband wound up employed at the same property. He had recently been promoted to maintenance supervisor, and she came to the office as administrative assistant. They had steady incomes, but nothing about their lives was easy. With their own small children to raise, Jessica was constantly pulled into the challenges posed by her mother's recurring difficulties, and then she discovered a younger sister she'd never known. At one point in time, she was also raising that sister's children because her sister was not competent to do so. Jessica had five kids under six years old in her care!

Shortly into her stint at that property, Jessica recognized that the property manager to whom she reported was not conducting himself professionally. She did the best she could to do her own work in spite of his behavior, but she soon found that to be yet another stressor in her life. After finding him sleeping in the office on multiple occasions, she made the difficult decision to report his behavior. While both her employer and the Board of Directors at the association supported her taking action, some property owners were not quite as understanding when the employer subsequently promoted Jessica to property manager. They voiced concerns about her relative inexperience, the potential complication of Jessica becoming the direct supervisor of her husband, and some became poised to find fault with almost any action she took.

"This was the first time I'd actually been a licensed property manager. I'd always been an assistant, so it was a lot of learning. A lot of hard work. And, it's tiring. It's really a 24/7 job. They say the business day is 8:00 to 4:00 o'clock, but almost everyone has my phone number—and they do not hesitate to use it. Any time there's a problem, it's mine to deal with."

Whenever Jessica tried to implement a new approach or policy, owners complained that she wasn't like the previous two managers, or even the one they all still raved about from twenty years prior. Then the aging property needed major renovation and a large construction project commenced. This added to Jessica's job exponentially—meeting with engineers, coordinating on-site inspections, and responding to owners' complaints about the construction crew and the property being in a state of constant upheaval.

"I don't like when there is something to be done and there is nothing that I can do about it. It seems like it's my fault that the construction going on is taking too long. It's really not my fault, but I take it on as if I need to find a way to finish it. When things don't go right and I have to notify people of the situation, in their minds, it's my fault."

She took it all on. While some owners complained about her methods, the Board President told her she was "as tenacious as a pit bull." She interpreted that as a compliment. Jessica would research something until she found the answer, no matter how long it took; she even dreamed about it until she solved the problem.

And, that was just her "day job!" Simultaneously, she and her husband started their own business to do handyman work and small construction projects in their "spare time." Her husband dreamt of having his own business his whole life, and Jessica was determined to help him fulfill that dream. No matter what it required.

"I don't know that either one of us was really prepared for how we were gonna do it, or prepared for how much time it would take. We're leaving work and driving to another community. How is this gonna be possible? We have to sleep!"

Jessica rarely had anything come easy, nor did she expect it to. Asked what kept her going in the times, she doubted herself and became reflective on all that she had endured.

"Everything I've been through, if I can get through all of that, I can get through this. My husband is a big support— kinda reminds me to 'take a breath.' We've been through worse. So, I go back and look at all those things."

Jessica went from high school, to the military, to office work, to manager, now to the uncertainty and relentless demands of business ownership. All while raising her own children and being the only glue holding her extended family together. Yet, her energy and tenacity prevailed.

Paul

It took a while for Paul to get into the groove of working for himself after all of the other paths he had tried. He stopped and started both in the business and his personal life more than a few times. When asked what he thought it took to make it in his field, he shared views about the hard road.

"You cannot be afraid to fail. You cannot be afraid to take risk. You cannot be afraid. It's not really being risk-averse. You just have to trust that it's your plan, it's going to come together because all your eggs are in the basket anyway. Trust in your plan, because if you don't have a plan, you've already failed."

Paul expounded further on self-talk and having confidence to figure it out, and the importance of a plan for the next thing. He also cautioned others who asked that they had to expect the entrepreneurial road to be tough.

"I tell anyone, don't get into this thinking it's easy. You can be the best tradesman in the world, but yeah, that doesn't make you a good businessman. Don't go into it thinking *I'm good at this*. Go in knowing that it must and will be hard. Nothing worth doing is easy. It must be hard. I tend to think when things are going well, my first thought is, *something's wrong*. Where's the hammer that's going to drop on my head? I'm waiting for the unexpected to happen."

He admitted he doesn't totally trust when things are going along smoothly. He thinks that someone is trying to take something from him. He shared that this feeling of foreboding used to make it impossible for him to sleep, but he noticed recently that he was getting better at going back to sleep. He speculated as to whether that's because he's getting older, or maybe things really are getting better. Maybe it's time to trust.

Ted

In Ted's early years, he could have been the poster child for taking the hard road. The story of being expelled has already been told. The logical choice would have been to find out then and there what it would take to get himself back into high school as soon as possible. But logic did not enter into that teenage brain. Ted described the time after expulsion as being filled with almost every conceivable menial job available at the time.

"I sold almost anything during the war (WWII). Collected, bundled, and rolled newspapers and magazines, foil went to scrap dealers. Iron and metal brought premium prices but was harder work. After that I set pins at the local bowling alley until my knuckles were so calloused and swollen that my fingers barely closed; cleaned bricks with a hammer and gloves—100 for $1.00—gloves had to be replaced frequently for thirty-nine cents. I dug graves and trimmed trees, cut and loaded firewood. With my then bulging muscles, I decided to take up boxing at the local Elks Club. Realizing the futility of it all, I luckily landed a full-time cleaning job at a local factory."

Factory life did not last long. Instead, he embarked upon nearly two years of short-term jobs, tough physical labor across thirty-seven states before figuring out that his choice to run away entailed too much effort for very little, if any, return. At one point in his journal, he admitted that the 1937 Chevrolet in which he and his buddy toured the US "ate up most of our earnings in gas and repairs."

The spirit of adventure propelled Ted and his friend through harvesting peas, selling souvenirs at rodeos, and laying railroad tracks. They could intersperse those jobs with a little bit of fishing and sightseeing. But at some point, he grew road-weary. After driving thousands of miles in one direction, he knew it was time to turn around and go back to where he left off.

"I had an awakening, or epiphany, realizing I should return to high school and hopefully college, to pursue a career."

Those early jobs taught Ted a great deal. He learned about hard work, how he did *not* want to spend his life, which brought him a new appreciation for education. Armed with the knowledge gained from those experiences, he began to figure out how to work smarter while he worked hard.

Chapter 5

Find and Cultivate a Team

*Surround yourself with people that push
you to do and be better. No drama or
negativity. Just higher goals and higher
motivation. Good times and positive
energy. No jealousy or hate. Simply bringing out the absolute best in each other.*
Warren Buffett

There are a plethora of sayings and idioms about the value of teamwork. In fact, it was a challenge, nearly impossible, to settle on one or two that best capture the essence of this theme. One often muttered by Ted's grand-son while working alongside him was, "teamwork makes the dream work," drawn from the title of the bestselling book by John C. Maxwell (Maxwell, 2002). Anyone who has worked in corporate America has sat through at least a half-dozen team-building seminars or interactive workshops to emphasize and facilitate the goal of developing effective teams to achieve shared outcomes. But consider the person starting out on his or her own, busy with the dozens of details of a startup or trying to eke out enough income to get through to the next paycheck. The likelihood of devoting time to obstacle courses or personality inventories is next to nil. And let's not forget, that once people come together to comprise a team, it then requires cultivation to keep the crew growing and working well together—an additional demand on an already busy leader or a novice entrepreneur.

The courage to get started is empowering. The first steps may feel bold and exciting. But sometimes, even for the most independent of adventurers—a glimpse of someone else on the path can be reassuring. A fellow hiker warning you of a blocked path ahead or advice to seek cover due to an incoming storm might relieve a weary traveler. Even for the person blazing their own trail, a little companionship along the way often brightens the journey.

It is fair to presume that the people in this book were interviewed, at least in part, because something about their *individual* paths seemed likely to reveal an interesting story. It was a true privilege to listen carefully and be brought into their worlds. Our questions focused on each individual's story, but almost inevitably, the need to seek out and surround oneself with others emerged as part of the stories they told. It may have been hiring staff with skill sets different from their own. For some, it was finding and consulting with advisors or groups that could act as a de facto board of directors. In other cases, it was actually the harsh truth or comment that cut to the core of the individual's weakness or hesitation that was enlightening. The key in each circumstance was recognizing the path could not be undertaken totally alone, that one individual could not possibly be competent in all the aspects of business that were necessary to move forward.

It became clear from the recollections shared that getting the right people on board was imperative. Yet seeking assistance is not simple. In most cases, the need arises while the business is in its fledgling stages. The concept of spending money on additional employees or outside consultants during startup can discourage someone from doing so when it might make the most difference to the organization. In other words, spending more to make more may feel very risky at the time. Risky, but wise.

Angie

Angie's role in real estate changed drastically in a short period of time. She started as an agent for another entity and then started her own company within just a few years. She explained in her characteristic high-energy, high-speed speech.

"I got my license in 2010, then shortly left one company and went to another. And when I went to the second company, it was like the whole world opened up to me, because my first company that I was with sort of made me feel like I was an employee. And the second company was like, 'No, no, no, you own your own business. Let us help you grow your business.' And I had never even considered that was an option. I was like, 'What do you mean?' And they were like, 'You can do whatever you want. You can do this. You can do that.'"

They made her realize she could be her own boss and be part of a team. This idea that she could do whatever she wanted was a brand-new concept for Angie. As a young woman, she bounced around ideas for learning and employment, both figuratively in her dreams, but also, literally across multiple college campuses. She did not assert direction or focus into any one area. "My mom suggested I become a secretary, teacher, or nurse—because those were the options offered to her. Nobody ever encouraged me and said you can do anything you want." Until decades later, when her current employer cultivated a sense of ownership in her, for her own business.

She now enjoys her own team of agents and employees that she nurtured, spurred on because her employer believed in her. This new team allows her to spend her time doing the aspects of the business that she likes the most and which utilize her areas of expertise the best. The freedom to devise her schedule accordingly is another benefit to surrounding herself with a good team.

"I have five people working and taking care of the business—I trust them with all of my life. My 'right-hand girl' is the other side of my brain. I have thoughts, ideas, and I just text her—she answers back almost immediately with 'I've got it.' I can do that from anywhere. I trust them, but I'm always checking in because I know I'm hyper-controlling."

Angie prefers to work with the seller side of real estate; the buyer role is one she has moved away from. So, she has a buyer's agent on her team who works with the buyers, does the open houses, and in some ways, feels like he's running his own business.

"I love helping him be his own boss. He's got a finance background and just loves competing with himself. There's no top-down thing there because he is so self-motivated to be productive."

Like some of the other people in this book, Angie works with her husband in the business. He joined once it was obvious that it was more than a whim, it was a serious enterprise with promising monetary outcomes. Angie's mother-in-law was one of a few who were not so sure about their arrangement.

"It was an interesting dynamic that I was the primary breadwinner in the family. She assumed I was going to be his assistant. That was the perception of her generation, and I do think it was hard for him early on, a bit of adjustment and negotiation. But now we work together and make the same amount of money. The great thing is that our skill sets are completely opposite. So we never step on each other's toes. I totally trust him. He totally trusts me. We come together to decide how it's going to work. I can't imagine hiring another graphic designer or marketing person—his content speaks for me. It looks like it's coming from me. He knows my voice better than anybody."

Tim

A disc jockey seems like a position that is, at its core, an individual endeavor. Tim has felt at times that it was important to stand out in the crowd and be a solo personality. On the other hand, he pointed out that in his particular creative enterprise, connecting with others also led to a synergy that was more energizing to the listener than what either entertainer alone could produce. Before Tim tried his hand at being a DJ in Las Vegas, his most rewarding experience in his hometown was working with a small group of peers to produce music-oriented parties. Those rather intimate performances led to professional gigs. The love of connecting with people over music is the passion that continued to drive him forward. While he described the environment as competitive, he also claimed that the creativity was unifying.

"I find that when I create something, that is what people want to align themselves with as well. That's probably opened more doors for me than anything else. Creating something that brings in a crowd leads you into more collaboration. I think that when people see that you're doing your own thing and you're self-motivated, collaboration comes after that."

Tim related a recent example of this when one of the DJs he subcontracts to contacted him. The DJ was asking Tim's advice about what rate of pay he should request for doing a particular guest spot. Tim sensed the guy's uncertainty and offered to collaborate.

"I said, 'Hey, how about we just make it a thing together? Let's just partner at this venue and see how it goes.' That's the best—assert yourself and then people will align with you. Creativity and assertiveness really make the wheel turn sometimes. It takes a willingness to partner and see someone else's vision and see it inside your own."

Tim strives to replicate the type of day-to-day association with other artists that he began with in his hometown, believing there is plenty of opportunity for this to happen. His upbeat approach to sharing artistry and success in a business that is often more cutthroat may yet lead to additional fruitful partnerships.

Laurie

The motivation for Laurie to seek out others to assist her was that, as hard as she tried, she couldn't do it all. That realization came to her during the first year of running her own business. She describes herself as "suffocating." She had a new baby, she and her husband had downsized their living arrangement to save money, she was meeting with potential customers to obtain more jobs, and working in the field. Overwhelmed, she turned to her mentor once again. He bluntly told her, "Hire someone."

Laurie was in disbelief at how simple he made it sound. She replied, "I can do that?" He shrugged his shoulders and said, "Put an ad out there and interview."

"I got smart. I did hire a bookkeeper. That was great. Then I started hiring more people to do the office tasks because I hated that stuff. I still hate it. Then I finally put myself through some coaching and leadership training. That really made a huge difference. I finally understood corporate structure. More recently, I've learned how to go from having twenty-seven employees all reporting to me, to just three. They are now the ones supervising large numbers of employees. The business became something different—no longer a small business—so I had to do it differently. I never got as big as Ted. That business had about ninety employees at one point."

In addition to hiring in-house, Laurie sought outside counsel, particularly once her first mentor was long out of the business. She found assistance and much needed support from other women in business.

"I always surrounded myself with smart people. I joined a group of women company presidents. They were like my board of directors. They convinced me that I needed someone to run my human resources. In hiring someone, I could stop listening to people whine about a day off or whatever other petty shit they had going on. Another time, when I was in a near financial crisis, those same women convinced me to hire a financial officer—told me I'd never make it otherwise."

Laurie credits those ladies as being instrumental in attaining a short-term loan to get out of debt. They gave her the name of a well-regarded expert who prepared her financial documents. Going into the loan presentation, she had little confidence that she would convince them that her company was worthy.

"After all, I was just another landscape company struggling. I could tell by the looks on their faces that they didn't think I knew what I was doing. I pulled out documents that the consulting expert had prepared, shared his name and said, 'His analysis shows there is no doubt that I can handle this cash flow.' I actually saw them sit up and pay attention."

Another time this pseudo board of directors made her come to a meeting and rehearse firing someone. When she stumbled on her words or was not direct during the rehearsal, they made her do it over again. A little wine and a lot of practice later, they declared her ready to do it on her own. Not only did she do it, she and the guy she fired are still friends. He found a job with a better fit and was grateful.

Laurie believes she could not have discovered solutions or made those difficult business decisions without those women coaching her.

"Yeah—surrounding myself with amazing people. God, I love them."

Chris

The painting business was growing nicely for Chris. He hired a few guys to do the majority of the painting while he did everything else. Chris loved being busy. He ran for supplies, scheduled the jobs, answered the phone, carried out all the correspondence, and quoted the next jobs. And he kept track of every detail on his phone. He excitedly gestured toward the screen on his phone, "I ran an almost million-dollar business on Google Notes. Notes on my phone for taxes, for numbers, for scheduling. The only thing that kept me held together was Google Notes."

Landing a much-desired commercial job, as well as his record-keeping strategy, threw him into a tailspin. It was a whole other level of demands. He coped the best he could but realized he couldn't keep going at that pace, something had to change. Much like Laurie, he was faced with the reality that he simply couldn't do everything any longer. He claims that hiring a business coach turned around his thinking.

"He started by recommending we make our lead foreman a Project Manager. He already knew that I trusted the foreman. Told me to think about incentivizing him, give him a raise, maybe he gets a vehicle. As I thought about it, it seemed right. He was the guy I could always count on, reliable, one guy I never had a problem with. He was down with it in two seconds, couldn't wait to do it. The next thing the coach told me was to get someone to do my customer interactions and scheduling. I had a woman doing social media part-time, and she was doing a great job. Another really reliable person, never had to chase her down or follow up."

That "woman doing social media" is now the person he relies upon for the tasks that previously bogged him down, the Program Ops Director. She has established a process for all the functions he previously executed via Google Notes. The fact that Chris brought her along on the interview made it clear that he relies on her day in and day out.

The business coach opened Chris's eyes to building a team. He guided him to build a structure to support the main functions of the business.

"We built a system with hierarchies. People can be held responsible for their part in the business, instead of me trying to do ninety percent of things. He was a huge help in that. I worked with him for like nine months, and it made a huge difference. And all my Google Notes are gone!"

Chris smiled as he described the relief he felt when these changes went into place. It felt freeing to him, and opened up time on his own agenda—time he needed to try his hand at the next thing on his wish list, acquiring real estate for rentals or for renovating and selling later. All because he opened himself up to the ideas of someone who knew more than he did about organizing people around a common goal.

Rachel

New hair stylists must establish themselves as talented in their own right. This came fairly easily to Rachel. She had interned with a highly regarded stylist and demonstrated her skills early on. But as an employee, she felt rather undervalued. Then with someone who offered a "partnership," that she did not feel was a true partnership, she felt duped. In fact, she described that experience as the worst agreement possible and one that taught her how she would do things differently. Her opportunity to create a team her way came once she was able to free her location from being the "sister" location to the main one. She could finally take action to create a pleasant and appealing atmosphere.

"I could focus on building our team, addressing what our staff needed and meeting our clients' needs at the same time. I was able to nurture that salon, able to grow it—have a really great culture, good people, and energy."

From the moment a customer contacts the salon, he or she gets the sense that the environment is lovingly created to make them and the employees comfortable. How else would you feel after being greeted on the phone with, "It's a great day at (XX) Salon!," or offered warm herbal tea as your coat is whisked away? The renovated house provides a cozy space in which to pamper and be pampered.

Rachel relates that being able to coach, seeing the stylists learn and grow, are amongst the favorite parts of her role. She fosters input from her management team because she knows that they have insights and see things that she may not. Likewise, she encourages them to care for their customers. She actively seeks customer feedback and follows up as needed.

External relationships are also important to Rachel's business. She lists a good accountant and a good bookkeeper as essential for keeping on track. Like Laurie, she has also sought out other business owners, particularly women business owners, from whom to learn and find commonalities.

"When I go to those classes, I really try to listen. A lot of people go because they want to hear themselves talk. But I want to hear what others have done and relate it to me, to my business. Would that work? Could I do it better? I learn at classes and from other bosses that I had. I want to be somebody that the team can come to trust and respect."

A testimony to Rachel's efforts was shared on social media not too long ago. The Facebook page for her business saluted her on Boss's Day. One of the fourteen stylists described her as a fierce leader.

"It is said that a good leader takes a little more than her share of the blame and a little less than her share of the credit. You live this every day . . . you allow us to work independently with confidence. Thank you for placing the trust in us to do the best work possible. We love you!"

From being initially discouraged by a counselor, at the risk of "ugly feet and a crooked posture," to her own thriving business with a supportive group surrounding her. Could there be any clearer indication of a well-functioning team?

Alexandra

Alexandra started her teaching business on her own, out of frustration with a system that she believed did not serve children in need of learning alternatives. Admittedly, she felt very much alone in the early days. She recalled not having the confidence in herself in a leadership role, but the drive to generate a solution spurred her on. She then began reaching out through various social media platforms and discovered others who were founders of similar programs. In fact, Alexandra's current lead teacher and occupational therapist came to her from that avenue, from searching for a group where she belonged. Alexandra began finding people by sharing her mission and her passion.

She came to realize that her mission was beyond teaching. It was to lead, be an entrepreneur, and create choices and options for families. As a teacher, she had a responsibility to foster the development in all learners, especially those who were neurodiverse. This was in stark contrast to the teachers she observed as a child, those who used their power to control. Her passion and commitment to the success of her students has allowed her to build a team based on mutual respect. They have grown, and Alexandra is able to delegate the instruction and shift her own emphasis because of that team. Her conviction is stronger now, having been a micro school for two years. She reminds us that academics and cognitive development are not the only keys to her students' success, but also growth in areas like self-management, communication, and safety. This goal, to provide holistic care to her students, is her solution.

"I love our team because each of us has an expertise, and although I'm the leader, the principal, we don't do hierarchies or anything like that. I recognize that each of them has an expertise, so anytime there's something I want to do, I put it out there. I ask the group, 'How do we do it?' Then I hear all the ideas and we make it happen. We are in a system, mainstream public education, that doesn't understand what the child truly needs... but if I believe that I can make a change, and make it happen, then I wanna do it."

Alexandra has also become a mentor to other founders of micro schools and joined additional social media groups that serve to inspire teachers and families searching for something new, something to take care of all of the needs of the children, not solely academic in nature. She values the connections she has made both for the support she receives and the opportunity to give back to a caring community of like-minded people. Thanks in part to its virtual configuration, her team is ever-expanding and can grow as large as she decides to make it. While it is often said that it takes a village to raise a child, Alexandra has literally created one—and all of "her kids" are certainly blessed by her perseverance and desire to cultivate her team.

Jessica

In the military, Jessica experienced the benefits of a collective approach to getting things done. Once out of that environment, gathering others around her was not an immediate priority. Until she became a property manager. Once in that role, it was an adjustment for Jessica to regard herself as boss. She obtained her Property Management Certification and the title, but she didn't want to ask anyone on her team to do anything that she wouldn't do. Instead, she let them know that she planned on being more than an administrator, she would be part of the working team to keep the property looking beautiful. As we talked, she shared her resistance to the idea of being the boss and emphasized the importance of teamwork.

"I'll do it—anything, you know, to help get it done. I'll help paint the decks. I'll help dig a hole, you know, I'll help do whatever. I'm not one to be telling everyone else, 'You do this or that.' I've never seen myself as a boss person! I've had bosses where it's like, 'do it, do it, do it.' I know you have to draw a line in my role, but I don't like it if I can't be part of getting things done."

Now, two years later, Jessica and her husband are still employed by property management companies but have also started their own contracting business. And for her, although he has more skills in the trades and hers are in the accounting area, she still wants it to be a partnership. Jessica and her husband are a team, co-owners, navigating something new together.

"It's been a leap of faith. Having his own business is something he's (her husband) dreamed of since he was fifteen. We weren't really prepared for how much time it was going to take and how little sleep we'd get. We leave our regular work and go work for someone else. But I'm learning everything. I've learned how to drywall, paint, totally learning on the job."

Jessica and her husband are partners and a team, working together for their family and to fulfill their dreams. The path is uncertain, as she herself said, a leap of faith. She is also quick to add that they have been through far worse, but her husband's encouragement to "take a breath...and you'll get through," has reminded her that the journey is worth it.

Mona

The idea to make body products from natural ingredients started as a solo endeavor. Mona sought out a panel of others to help turn her project into reality. She first tried an all-natural deodorant and shared it with friends. Mona also joined a group of like-minded entrepreneurial women who pushed her to start the company. At a retreat, the other attendees encouraged her to start selling the products to other folks. It started with website development to establish a basic market presence. She added more lines such as lip balm and body butter, and got them into the hands of local shop owners. Not long after, a local breast cancer advocacy group began endorsing the products. Mona began to see the benefits of wider distribution and word of mouth. Hearing that the lip balms and deodorant were helping people drove her forward.

Until very recently, Mona's work to develop and market self-care products remained a solo endeavor. She employed one woman part-time to complete specific tasks, such as developing email lists, writing her blog, and sending out newsletters. She's also occasionally hired people to do social media, but that has not always worked out as she'd hoped. Then, recently, Mona decided it was time to slow down, due to a health problem.

The decision has not discouraged her. She still wants to grow her business organically, describing herself as being very 'calculated.' A local cancer center has endorsed her products, and that's an important step. She has plans underway to begin to have others contribute to the enterprise. Her husband is going to come on board part-time in the fall and help her with sales. The plan is for him to track down the possible clients, allowing Mona the time to go sell.

She has also found a woman-owned business in another state. It is a small-batch manufacturer that may be able to take on some of Mona's production tasks.

"I've been doing everything myself. Making the product in a kitchen attached to my house, putting the stickers on, marketing. It's a lot, and in the last year I'm still trying to figure out how to really grow the company because I can't sustain working the way I am and trying to grow it. I'm having this company test out making the products and developing a price structure. Hopefully, I can transition to them because I can't continue."

Mona is at a critical decision-making point. She has lofty goals but is feeling her own limits. The inroads she has made individually are impressive and admirable. A clear path to expanding her team may be the next step to making her dreams reality.

Ted

Two goals drove Ted's decision-making. He wanted more than anything to have his own business—a thriving, influential landscape business. And he wanted to support his family. That meant the usual expenses incurred by a family, but also paying for Janice (his cherished wife) to attain her dream—get a college degree and be able to teach young children. She had stood by his side during his service years, throughout his horticultural studies, and by fulfilling the bookkeeper role before he could afford to pay for that expertise. It was time for him to help make her goals a reality as well. This was no small task. It took three jobs for Ted to make this work.

To juggle all three, team building and networking became crucial. As gardener and caretaker at an upper-class, waterside estate on Lake Ontario, Ted earned housing for his family. At that location, he also made the acquaintance of many well-to-do homeowners needing landscape expertise that his fledgling tree and landscape company could provide. An attorney who lived along this so-called "Gold Coast" of Rochester became his lifelong advisor on legal and real estate matters, a trusted collaborator. Not wanting to wait on his goal of ownership while tending the rolling estate, he hired two high school friends who had also pursued horticultural degrees following their years in the Korean War. They were the landscape team that formed the foundation for the company bearing his name.

These high school friends and loyal employees picked up more responsibilities when Ted began his work as tree supervisor at the country club. They took on the horticultural side, while Ted tapped into people around him with expertise in the other areas he needed.

"Brother Donald did some of his artwork magic and developed characters for marketing while my friend, Dan, who was a 'public relations genius' connected me to marketing resources." Ted often tapped into family and friends to be part of his team through the years, including his aging father.

Once his father retired from full-time work, Ted hired him to oversee smaller jobs. Ted's memoirs note that he was "stunned with Dad's vitality and interest" and that much like when his father smoothed things over after his high school expulsion, his father stepped in again as a voice of reason in a contentious situation. "His diplomacy and tact saved my ass and preserved my reputation." Ted had clashed with the high-power landscape architect of an important client, but his father's mild, cooperative nature helped reach a compromise.

Eventually, Ted was able to quit the country club position and focus full-time on building his business. He never shied away from hiring more talent, bringing on landscape architects, foremen, and sales staff. At one point, he went to the local community college and hired five new graduates to add to the company. Building the business to make more money meant spending even more on employees; on specialized team training, and on incentivizing the staff to perform to the best of their ability. A former employee shared that Ted sought out ways to make those around him smile with his poems, silly song lyrics, and teasing antics. He even had an ongoing wager with all of his employees—a sort of "Stump Ted" (pun totally intended). Simultaneously taking great pride in his vast ability to identify all varieties of plants while striving to develop a similar knowledge among his employees, he promised twenty dollars to any employee who could find a plant that he could not name.

Ted made a point of asking his employees for their opinions and inquiring about their areas of interest and desire for growth. At one point, his efforts earned him accolades in the local newspaper for giving employees a voice in company management. He formed a group, dubbed "The Green Team," of representatives from each of his company's departments that met with him regularly—without their direct supervisors being present. His emphasis on individual and team development was rare in the landscape world of the 1970s but yielded rewards for all involved over the course of those years.

Chapter 6

Knowing When to Change Direction

Perhaps some detours aren't detours at all. Perhaps they are actually the path.
Katherine Wolf

I t is said that change is constant. Seasons change. Modes of transportation have changed. Technology, both our access to and use of it, have profoundly changed. Yet while some people seem to thrive on these permutations over time, perhaps even instigate them, others cringe and lament even the smallest deviation from what is familiar and comfortable. A new operating system? A new phone? An unanticipated detour on your road trip? Does that excite you or make you roll your eyes?

Whether one believes change and disruption are inevitable or not, our interviewees clearly articulated that being both willing and able to learn as you go, respond to bumps in the road, and recognize when it is necessary to take another direction are attributes absolutely necessary to "make it" in their fields. Interestingly, adapting to the COVID-19 pandemic was one example that several provided when asked about challenges that led them to change.

Change might bring a realization of the need to seek help in learning new strategies, planned or unplanned. An openness to learning along the way, either through structured approaches or "building the plane as it flew," was prevalent in our interviewees' stories. This attitude toward learning helped those new to a field or to operating a business ramp up their own modus operandi. Whether they sought formal learning opportunities or learned by the "school of hard knocks," none of them shied away from, nor minimized, the significance of continuing to learn.

Laurie

There were two times that changes in the national economy caused Laurie and her business managers to be very stressed. In 2008, and again in 2011, the plummeting stock market and an economy in recession impacted her landscape business.

"Most companies like ours were laying off employees in the middle of the summer. We weren't doing that. We took a divide-and-conquer approach. We reduced employees' hours to 33 so we were able to keep them on our books. Somehow, we did really well. Then, again, in 2011, business went down really fast."

Laurie attempted to continue with a comment about being stressed throughout that time period, but faltered. A pained grimace crossed her face, underscoring her fraught experiences. Regaining her composure, she quickly related the problem resolution. She learned to rely on advisors.

They encouraged her to change the way she was doing things. Based on their input, she adjusted her business model before things got any worse.

As she related in Chapter 3, when Laurie entered the landscape world, it was decidedly a male-dominated field. Hiring a woman at that time was unheard of. Fast forward a couple of decades, and talk about a different direction! In Laurie's company, her whole leadership team is female.

With a wry chuckle, she proclaims, "It wasn't on purpose. For a while, I felt kind of guilty that I couldn't get any guys to step up to my expectations. It seems like, maybe it's just this industry, but it's hard to find men who can multitask. If possible, I try to have one man and one woman assigned to every job, but it doesn't always work out that way."

She considers it to still be an industry problem, that most companies, when she attends meetings, continue to primarily hire white men. After describing the whole situation as feeling "bizarre" to her in this day and age, an adamant tone underscores her next point.

"I'll tell you something, our women employees definitely outrun (the men), I think because women want to prove themselves. They definitely want to prove that they can do it, that it's not a man's business. And, we've proven that it's not. It's a for-everybody business."

Laurie was willing to embrace change during tough economic times. Embracing alternative approaches may have saved her business. She also hired in keeping with her own high expectations, regardless of others' practices. In doing so, her company brought a whole new profile to the industry because of those expectations.

Chris

Chris believes having a sense of when to change direction is important. He spoke about a time in his business that he felt like he kept making the same mistakes over and over. After consulting with an advisor and stopping to analyze, he realized he was expecting an extremely high level of performance from employees, and they were not living up to his standards. It became apparent that unless they had some sort of stake in the business, his expectation was unrealistic. He had to do something about it, learn from his mistakes, and do things differently. He related an analogy that helped him see the need to change. When he recalls that time compared to now, he feels much better.

"Sometimes it felt like death by a thousand paper cuts. If you're getting cut over and over by the red paper, that's a problem, because you're not learning. But if it's of different colored paper, now you don't really have a problem because you already learned to avoid that one. Yeah, if you keep getting cut by the same color paper, every single time, that's on you. On the other hand, if the cuts come from every color of the rainbow, as long as you're not repeating the rainbow again, you're probably gonna be okay. But you know, you know you're not repeating the same thing over and over and over. It's okay."

Knowing when it's time to change direction is a lesson that Chris learned, only after a series of repeated mistakes. Whether it was stubbornness, lack of confidence, or misreading a situation, it was the realization of the need for change that took him in another direction. This lesson learned, described here by Chris with vivid imagery, suggests that experience truly is the mother of invention!

Rachel

Rachel is grateful to the parent company with which her hair salon is aligned. From the time she embarked upon her affiliation with them, there was essential training in daily aspects of managing a business that she had not received in any previous setting. She took advantage of plenty of opportunities to take their courses in budgeting and financial planning. So when the world was hit with the COVID pandemic, she was relieved to again access their resources. This time, however, it simply was not enough, considering the profound challenges imposed upon her and her staff. The demands on a business requiring such close personal contact with its customers were enormous. Listening to a giant international enterprise give her advice about strategies such as holding off on paying your bills and keeping any cash received was downright frightening. In spite of the passage of years, Rachel teared up as she spoke about that time.

"They were very supportive, but after three months of not knowing what is going to happen day to day, or when we might be able to reopen, it was still hard. And the topics of COVID, quarantine and social distance? It's been four years now, but I definitely feel PTSD (post-traumatic stress disorder) on the anniversary of the imposed shutdown when these things are talked about. It's a feeling of not having control of your life."

Rachel had never been someone who watched the news, but COVID-19 changed her forever. She realized she needed to be aware every single day, because business was not going back to anything close to usual. The one word she used repeatedly to describe that time was "weird."

And it changed the nature of her business forever. For example, her hair salon is now open seven days a week and uses an array of different and innovative scheduling options that originated during the pandemic. There could not be as many people in the salon at one time due to social distancing, so they spread out the schedule. The result? Now, she encourages flexible scheduling routinely. And while, prior to COVID, customers typically had Saturday off, it was the busiest day for hair appointments. It is far from the busiest today. Her customers can now be seen across an array of times and days; they are available more days than Saturday for personal appointments. There are upsides to this and downsides as well.

"There's never really a day to turn off, unless it's a major holiday. Even though it may be Sunday, I still talk to my staff. It's hard because I feel like I just don't get a day off. Everything is just so accessible all the time; it never goes away. Still, it's a blessing because I can be at the kids' games or whatever."

COVID was not the only thing that instigated change in her world. Trends in hair style that influence schedules and inventory are ever-evolving.

"New techniques—like balayage (a specific, artful approach to hair color). That changed a lot. It stretched out the time between people's appointments, but then also their appointment time is longer. It has taught us that you need to be able to flex—probably in any industry—with the changes, or you will just phase out."

Another example of Rachel's need to change and be responsive to the external demands was the imperative to keep up with social media. She didn't really like that side of the business but knew it must be done. One strategy she tried was assigning another staff member to spearhead that effort. But the pace of change necessary for a media presence doesn't let up. She's still seeking the best path to address those demands.

"We need to constantly generate new ideas for our online presence without being repetitive. We must be innovative and have quality photos. I've had people take the role on, but it doesn't seem to last."

A pandemic, evolving trends, and the explosion of social media have pushed Rachel and her business to learn and to change. What will be next? She ponders new ideas in business models or the possibility of collaborating with others in the personal care industry to benefit one another's flow of clients. Whether those concepts—or others we've not yet seen—take hold, it is her response as a leader to the forces in the environment that have facilitated growth and development for her employees and her business as a whole.

John

John spent his entire professional career in sales. He considers his enthusiasm as the catalyst toward financial freedom and professional success. His smile, eye contact, and confident nature exude this exuberance in a natural and authentic manner. This behavior isn't just lip service— it is who John is. A lifetime in sales has led John to promote a variety of products, but his approach is consistent over time. He told us about using this energy and engagement in his role as a sales person.

"Be enthusiastic about your product, about yourself, because at the end of the day, you're selling yourself. They did a study on insurance, and it is the hardest thing to sell in the world, but it's what everyone needs and the people that buy, they buy it from people they like. So, in sales, success is based on your ability to be personable, being able to interact with people and have them like you, but also having the confidence in your product, having the confidence in yourself to go out there and sell."

Those qualities create opportunities for survival in sales. He emphasized that learning to pivot and adapting to change are crucial in sales, not only for survival but for rising above the rest in a very competitive industry. John described this in a story about sales numbers, called "activity"—similar to measuring productivity in any other workplace, where the time spent on a task translates into billable hours. High activity suggests the salesperson is successful, meeting sales goals, and on track for meeting or exceeding the standard. Low activity suggests one is missing the mark, and in a competitive sales market this could mean losing an established territory, or even worse, the job altogether.

He stated, "In sales, it's a numbers game. You are measured by your 'activity,' so you have to learn from your mistakes. And I make a lot of mistakes!" He laughed as he revealed this about himself. He continued, "That's okay as long as you learn from them and adapt. There is a book called *Who Moved My Cheese?* and it talks about the ability to adapt (Johnson, 1998). Some of the salespeople that can't adapt to new situations and change are not going to be successful. You have to be able to change and roll with the punches and think on your feet and get it done."

It is his enthusiasm, positivity, and adaptability that has facilitated John's success in sales for over twenty years. Would his enthusiasm be enough to carry him? Would a "can-do" attitude allow him to rise above the challenges of the inevitable changes on the path ahead? Time and time again, John turned to books, from his father or others he found on his own, as sources of wisdom and guidance. John was armed with tools that helped him not only navigate change, but embrace it. Tools that thus far, have served him well.

Alexandra

Alexandra revealed her views on change when she was asked about the qualities it takes to be able to take the type of risk that she did—going from a secure, employed position to initiating her own learning enterprise. School districts are often regarded as ideal places to work because of the built-in time off, the stability of the job market, and the benefits. Yet Alexandra gave up that security and assessed what it took to take a dramatic turn along the way.

"You have to be open to reinvent yourself. You have to be open to change. And be willing to change even when it's your own short- or long-term goals. Those might swivel and switch. I think you have to believe in what you want, believe in yourself. For me, I've had to learn how to believe in myself. If I fall, I will get back up, dust myself off, and keep going. Because there is a bigger mission, there's a bigger purpose, and I have a bunch of kids I'm advocating for. So I have to stay focused, resilient, and be open to change and learn in the process."

Alexandra doesn't think that what she has done is anything special or anything deserving of recognition. For her, it is more of an internal drive to change and evolve.

"I learned that *I* have to believe in the value of what I do. This is what I want to do, and I'll do it regardless (of what others think). I will make it happen. Believe in what you want and be open to change and to learn in the process."

Alexandra is not only in the business of learning, she directs her business by learning and changing. She admitted that the financial aspects of the business were not her strength. "My personal finances were not in a place where I could get loans, and that was a big challenge. Sometimes I wonder, did I make a mistake? Like, should I have waited until maybe I was in a better financial position to start this business? I was almost evicted from my house when I started, because of not being able to cover my personal finances while building the school enrollment. I had family members say, 'You're crazy.' I had a higher probability of failure than success."

She relies upon her strength, resilience, and the willingness to learn and pivot as she develops substantial goals for how she can grow and adapt in the future. She truly believes her future success, and that of her students, will depend on her willingness to continue to modify her path, her strategies, and her goals.

Shawn

Learning to communicate was a turning point in his life, his growth, and his actions. Shawn readily shared that early on in his career path, he tended to ignore or shut off potential problems. He recalls one of his biggest challenges being a notification from his bank that he was in deep financial trouble. His assets were being frozen related to a tax issue. An issue he'd ignored for too long.

"I just developed the ability to shut it off and not care about what happens next. I thought it was the only way to get through it, to be honest."

Who hasn't shut off or turned away from unpleasantry? Especially in younger years, many of us think if we just ignore it, it will go away. But as maturity sets in and the problems grow, so do the consequences of disregarding responsibility.

"The turning point in my life was when I learned to communicate. Instead of running or shuffling aside, I realized communication is the key. There was a guy who'd mostly given me bad advice, but I remembered something else he'd said. He told me that if I had just 'manned up' and responded to the first notices, my problems might have been more workable. If you owe a certain amount, maybe if you fess up and negotiate, it can be worked out. There is a lot less ill will than when shutting a guy off. As I think about it now, I screwed up. I should have just owned up to my situation."

Shawn reeled off a list of examples of how this lesson helped him. This change in attitude has helped with customers and in his personal life. He learned that there is tremendous relief that follows being accountable for your actions.

"It's rejuvenating—a lot easier to tell the truth, right? One of those things I should have listened to as a little kid. You want to do people right. And I learned it late. It feels good to be in a restaurant or at Home Depot, see someone, and not have to turn your head away or go down another aisle to avoid them. It feels good to hold your head up high. It took me too long."

His story emphasizes that it's never too late to learn to do the right things, to take the high road. Shawn turned an embarrassing, demoralizing experience into a life lesson that he lives by, and has passed on whenever he has a chance. The little changes, such as redirecting one's own behavior, are not so little.

Paul

Paul did not hesitate even a moment when asked to describe a challenge he encountered and how he overcame it: the pool of potential employees totally drying up was the force that required Paul to figure out a way to survive during change. Prior to COVID, he had twenty employees. After? He was down to six. Even two years later, the prospects were slim. Paul was forced to go back to being directly involved in the construction end, rather than over seeing his employees' work. Returning to hands-on construction was not the direction he wanted to go, but it became his motivation to pivot.

"It gave me an opportunity to think outside the box. I used to have no problem getting employees—put out an ad and I'd get ten calls. That wasn't happening anymore, every-one needed help. I started looking in big cities, like Atlanta, New York City. I even started offering to relocate people. That took more investment and more trust. Getting through it was very scary. Thank God that the PPP (Payroll Protection Plan) came out, because it was costing a huge amount of money."

It took another two years for Paul to build up his production workforce. He also credits this scary time with teaching him an important lesson that he continues to carry with him.

"I came to understand what is really important. My people. My workforce now is far more efficient and more productive. I invested in getting good people, invested in them and I've gotten my return on investment back. It tested me and gave me confidence, because I figured out how to make it work. I learned that I'll take a temporary margin hit to get good workers."

That new orientation toward investing in the people who drive the work of his company has led to yet another innovative approach for Paul. He realized that for many of his valued workers, English is a second language. When he would drive from location to location to be sure things were running smoothly, he could not be confident that he was being understood by them. It dawned on Paul that a translator might be the answer to this latest potential challenge to efficiency. Fortunately, a spouse of one of his workers was fluent in both languages.

"So, yeah, she's now on the books as an administrative assistant. She's a translator! She rides with me. She's my co-pilot, and it works out far better. I was hesitant at first, but I got her, and thank God. Got rid of the language barrier—so smart—like day and night; getting the right people."

Since returning to his overseeing role, Paul can concentrate on his next goal. He wants to grow the business to another level, be an organization. The plan is to build an infrastructure to be where he hopes by the end of 2025. He no longer worries about the day to day and is focused on the future.

Mona

Changes in the upper ranks at her engineering firm brought about a change in Mona's role. A new CEO was brought in to manage the company, and he was an expert in business development. Mona had wanted out of the engineering side due to her inability to pass the exam required for her licensure. She was far more interested in the development side. She was about to find a path away from the licensure problem dangling over her head and toward something more fulfilling.

"I asked if the new CEO would be my mentor. He agreed. We brought in a very big job and it was my lead. It was a game changer for the company. He told me once that happened, that I'd found my role and didn't need to worry about that engineering exam anymore—'This is your role. This is your baby.' Right after that, I became a partner. It was one of the biggest things in my professional life."

Mona acted upon a company change. Some might have considered it a step backward, but not her. By requesting a change in mentor, she changed her career trajectory. It wasn't the last time that Mona would act upon an opportunity to head in another direction. Fast forward to the months before starting the self-care products. It was personal changes that altered her journey this time around. Her tone changed to one of introspection and her voice softened as she described that time.

"So, now I'm 54. I'm in menopause. All these things are happening in my body. Nobody has answers for me. I find out I have osteoporosis, even though I'm doing everything I'm supposed to do, and I have to see a bone specialist, one who recommends medication. I'm thinking more about my body chemistry and nutrition, and they're telling me to start taking harsh medications? I'm not going to do it. Tell me about minerals. That I'll do. They tell me to have my sister get tested. She'd already had breast cancer, now I have to tell her to do this? She did and she has it also—so then we know it's hereditary. I'm ready to learn about all of that, that's what I'm going to keep diving into."

The passion for developing self-care products comprised of all natural ingredients is inherent to everything that Mona is now doing. The changes in her own body and that of her beloved sister have led her to redirect her energies from a hard-earned position as partner in a large company to making lip balm in her specialized kitchen. She is fascinated by the myriad of learning opportunities ahead of her as she develops more products and navigates challenges of the market.

Ted

Ted sold his beloved and successful landscape business after forty years dedicated to beautifying the Rochester region. He and Janice decided together that it was time to retire, enjoy family, and find a winter retreat where he could fish and they could enjoy fun in the sun. They both knew he would need to do more than that to keep busy, but he counted on letting time determine solutions.

Not long after he phased out of the final days of executing the transition of ownership, Ted was contacted by a public relations firm working with the festival organizers of Rochester's renowned Lilac Festival. They were seeking someone to sell lilacs at the festival and thought he would fit the bill. Ted was enamored of the idea as evidenced by this description: "My entrepreneurial nature was titillated." The short-term commitment and minimal tent fee enticed him to agree to a one year trial. Because he had a non-compete agreement with the landscape business that continued to hold his name, he and the public relations firm brainstormed name ideas, and rejected many before settling on one he (and his family) initially thought to be corny and presumptuous.

"Doc Lilac" was born! It attracted attention and caught on quickly. At nearly the same time, his old high school friend (referred to earlier as a "public relations genius") revived a previously defunct business selling lilac perfume and body lotion. They soon agreed to jointly promote the lilac plants and scented products. As the lilac sales increased over the next couple of years, so did the fees to have a tent at the festival. It was time to change direction and sell lilacs from the twelve acres surrounding his home. Not only did he save on his costs, but his whole family pitched in to help sell as the sales steadily increased. Following an item in a plant magazine about his lilac expertise, *Better Homes and Gardens* magazine sent a crew to interview Doc.

"All hell broke loose then, encouraging us to set up a website and sell online. The following year was the busiest of my life! My friends in public relations schemed relentlessly to keep me busy."

As an aside, Ted could not have been any less tech savvy. When his journal relates "we" set up a website, it was his public relations person who set it up, then his grandson and granddaughter-in-law who maintained the site, downloaded all of the orders, processed payments, and got the lilacs safely packaged for shipping. He needed lots of family support from the next generation to adapt to the change to an online business, but it served him well. He liked the ideas and the acclaim this career switch brought, while his loved ones became his copilots and crew.

The attention garnered from the national magazine feature led to yet another development. Ted ended up sending lilacs to Martha Stewart! As if this wasn't enough of a promotional tool, his friend who sold the perfume decided they should team up and send perfume and fresh-cut lilacs to the six living First Ladies (Laura Bush, Hillary Rodham Clinton, Barbara Bush, Roslyn Carter, and Betty Ford). Great idea, but it was no small task to keep fragile lilacs fresh during shipping. This endeavor attracted quite a bit of attention and was widely covered first by local, and then national, news outlets.

The Doc Lilac phase of Ted's adventure kept him vital for many years to come. From 1991 until 2016, it took Ted and three other people working to address both in-person and online sales during those busy spring months. After that time, the demands of aging began to take their toll, but he sure had found enjoyment during those years of change, when everything in his life was positively purple.

Chapter 7

Perseverance and Positivity Prevail

It's not whether you get knocked down,
it's whether you get up.
Vince Lombardi

Merriam-Webster's definition of perseverance is "the continued effort to do or achieve something despite difficulties, failure, or opposition." Whether one hits a bump in the road, encounters a detour, or discovers some other challenge along the journey, the persevering person continues on to reach their goal. And why not? Giving in to failure would leave you nowhere, except part way.

This quality emerged in many of our stories, sometimes by the teller specifically using the word *perseverance*, or by implying it within a personal philosophy or mindset about failure. Initially, perspectives on failure seemed somewhat contradictory. One view shared was that "failure was not an option," either because of a positive mindset or the fear of failing. Another was "be prepared for failure—it's inevitable, happens every day." Paradoxical, right? Yet, once these responses were further contemplated, it became apparent they are actually different ways of expressing an attitude about failure that, in either case, worked to propel the interviewee forward. By persevering in the face of failure, the efforts of the storytellers prevailed.

Jeremy

Jeremy landed with a firm that expected him to make cold calls. He found himself in a cubicle with a telephone book and the instruction from the owner of the firm to call people and make fifteen appointments a week. Being the same goal-oriented guy that recruited more friends into the Marines than anyone else had done, Jeremy made twenty-five. Somewhat unbelievably, he didn't even know what the company did, what needed to happen at those appointments.

Amused at his own product naivete, he revealed, "I finally asked and found out that we were selling long-term care insurance. So, I'm twenty-five years old, working with people to get them to buy nursing home insurance."

He ignored that irony out of desperation for an income. What he still didn't know, was that if he wanted to remain in the financial services arena, he would need to face one of his biggest fears—taking tests.

"When I was in school, I did a good job, but I couldn't take tests. I mean, probably the worst test-taker that ever lived. So, once in finance and insurance, I had to get all these exams, take investment exams. Take them before I could make any money, right? I needed money, I was so much in debt, with a wife and little baby. So, I just took it. I took it and failed. Seven times. And, each time, you have to go to a different city to take it. Every weekend, off I'd go, driving a few hours to take the test in a different place. Only when my father said, 'I'm going with you,' did things change. He went and sat in a chair outside the door so I could see him. That time, I passed!"

Seven times, seven cities before he finally passed. What was different on that seventh try? Maybe it was that he had six previous attempts to help him prepare, or maybe it was that his father insisted on coming along and remaining in the waiting area while Jeremy struggled through the test. Maybe that hard-earned support from his father helped Jeremy persevere.

When asked what kept him going through that time, kept him taking the test over and over, his reply was that it was a "fear of failure." He shared that his experience with his first business made that fear even more deeply ingrained.

"I feel that my first business was a failure. Now, I realize that *I* didn't fail—it was a failed business. It was a failure because I had a net loss when I sold the business. So, I said I will never fail again. I'm always going to succeed."

Fear of failure or a resolve to succeed? Jeremy continued to set goals, persevere, and use that combination of fear and resolve.

Angie

A far different view of failure was revealed during Angie's story. She was diagnosed with attention deficit disorder (ADD) at age fifty-four. Contrary to how she felt before the diagnosis, it revealed to her that she was not a failure. She slowly sipped her iced coffee, becoming quiet, contemplative, and reflective. She spoke carefully, as if giving advice to her former self.

"I would have loved to have known that I had ADD when I was nineteen, because I spent years beating myself up about not being smart. Turns out I am pretty smart. I'm just not a typical learner. And I think I would have probably set higher goals for myself as a younger person, you know. Growing up I went to a really good high school, I mean, all my friends went on to Harvard, Yale, you know, all the big schools, they all went to med school or to law school. And I just felt like, 'What's wrong with me, why can't I do that?' You know, it turns out that most of them are unhappy, because their parents made them do something they didn't want to do. Or they left their first career and now they're off doing music, you know what I mean? I guess we all end up where we're supposed to, but it's tough. It's tough when you're young and you're watching everybody else do these things and you don't have a goal. So, this (success as a realtor) was an accident. It was a total accident, but it was a good accident. I love it. I love it."

She uses this view when she gives advice to people just coming into the field. Angie suggests that people going into real estate not let a fear of failure or of being a failure hold them back. Perhaps it is that she had tried many other paths first, or because she defied the odds when she first got started.

Angie has come to believe in herself, trust her team, and in that new mindset, failure is not an option. "The truth is, every morning I get up unemployed. I don't have anyone tell me what to do today—essentially, I could lose my job tomorrow. There's no security, no tenure, there's nothing. So, you have to be passionate. If you wake up in the morning waiting for the phone to ring, you're never going to be successful. When I started, there was this statistic that only one in ten makes it through their first year in real estate. And of those people that make it through the first year, only one in four makes it through the next five years. When you're new in real estate, no one wants to talk to you because you're not going to be around in a year. I worked with three women who, for whatever reason, took me under their wing and taught me so much. They were so, so great to me."

So, once she got past that six- or seven-year mark, Angie wanted to help others get started.

"I started trying to help younger agents, and I did a lot of teaching. When I meet them, I always say, 'Look, I know you're terrified. You think you don't know what you're doing, but you do. You'll get there. And no one's gonna die.' The best advice I ever got was from my first office manager who said to me: 'Real estate is not neuroscience. If you fail, no one's gonna die.' Okay, so the pressure's off. Then my parents were my first clients. And they said, 'We don't care if the deal falls apart, we'll still love you.'"

The pressure may have been reduced by those words of advice, but it doesn't mean Angie takes any of it lightly. She keeps her role in perspective, yet prides herself on being an important person in people's lives. A supporter and guide of sorts when they are in the midst of life change.

Tim

Tim had been on the music path since early on. He clearly loved how it fueled his creativity and the ability to make connections. Beyond his passion of doing something creatively rewarding, he believed it also takes persever-ance and the right frame of mind.

"You have to want to do it. You have to want to do it every single day. You can look at the talented mega stars that are doing things, and it looks like the money comes to them easy, right? But at one point, they were the person that had to go out and find the gig, had to go out and ask people for a shot. That's what it takes to make it."

Tim filled in other details about specific celebrity names that he has followed over the years. They provided role models, but he quickly returned to the idea of perseverance.

"It takes responsibility to get up every single day and want to go do it, and want to go after it. You can't let down. That's the biggest part. You got to get up and do it."

There is no doubt about Tim's perspective here. His tone of voice and repetition of themes indicates he wants this message of perseverance to be shared again and again.

Chris

A positive attitude, one that accepts adversity as part of everyday life in business, was also Chris's outlook. This attitude was integral to every story he told about his child-hood experiences, it now is embedded in his business pathway, and he tries to instill it in his own employees. He believes this outlook is what gets him through the "grind," as he frequently describes his work travails.

"You gotta know you're gonna get overwhelmed. You're gonna get stressed out. It's gonna be a regular occurrence. You have to be able to do that for a long period, initially for years. You have to be okay with that, you have to accept it. A lot of people want it in six months, a year—quick. It doesn't ever happen. If it does, it usually comes back down as fast as it went up."

Even with that attitude and knowledge integral to his nature, Chris found himself at his wit's end about three years ago. He had taken on a commercial painting job for a very large construction company. It was the first time his business had ever ventured out of the realm of residential painting, where they had established themselves. He explained that commercial contracts are "notoriously tough." But he was convinced that it would not be that way for him. His positive attitude went even further—he was sure that his "little painting company" would do it differently, would handle the typical problems without difficulty. He was certain he would sail through it all smoothly—and admits today that others were laughing at his attitude. Reality hit him hard.

"I kept telling all my people—we're gonna do it. But we didn't, we struggled our asses off, we ran through people, stressed everyone out. It's the first time I'd ever cried because of the business. I called my foreman; I was stressed out of my mind. I said, 'Dude, I don't know if I can do this anymore.' He told me to go home, get some rest, and we'd figure it out the next day. I went home, talked to my wife, cried it out for a bit. I didn't think I could continue to do it; I thought it would send me to an early grave. She listened, and told me, 'Do what you gotta do, but we have these three boys and they can't have you like this.' Something had to change."

Chris had been through really tough times as a child, been in a lot of bad situations as a teen and young adult, had even gotten his business off the ground with no prior experience. But that new challenge, in a part of the business that he hadn't navigated before, knocked him down. Knocked him down for a short while. Then, the knowledge that his family needed him, and the families of his employees needed him to figure things out, led him back to his own philosophy. He knew that getting through this commercial contract was going to be formidable, but he put his head down to grind yet again.

John

John recalled many examples of being responsible at a young age. These instances likely influenced his outlook on life.

"At seven I came home alone from school, while my parents were still at work, until like seven or eight o'clock at night. So I had to be responsible on my own. Do my homework. Get meals. And by the time I was ten, I was babysitting kids in my building. By thirteen I was a camp counselor, and then when I was eighteen, I decided to go into the military."

Wow. These early examples of a self-proclaimed "disciplined child," also imply a much deeper story that goes beyond responsibility. John's early adaptive behaviors evolved into an adult who does not give up. No matter the circumstances. A college friend once told John that he was too positive. He wasn't sure if that was a criticism or a compliment! John credits his father for instilling that attitude.

He says this about his father:

"My dad always had a positive attitude. I never heard that guy complain. He got me this book called *You Can't Afford the Luxury of a Negative Thought*, by Peter

McWilliams, and I read that book (McWilliams, 1997). It said if you think you can do it, you can and you will. But if you think you can't, you definitely won't. I had to learn to believe in myself, knowing that sometimes failure was not an option. You gotta be able to adapt to change, and you gotta figure it out … but failure is not an option." John credits the book and his new mindset as making a profound impact on his life.

Ever since, he has lived by having a positive outlook. He recalled being assigned a territory as a sales representative, in an area totally unknown to him, at a time when he was trying to support his family of five on his income alone. John had moved the family for this job and was finding his way into what was essentially a start-up.

"I got into a pharmaceutical sales job where I had to do a business start. Typically, the territories are already established when a salesperson comes in. They are in place because some doctors are already prescribing, but not this one. No one was prescribing, it wasn't established, and so it was very difficult to kind of get it off the ground. It took me so long. After months and months of almost zero sales, it's like, you know what, what do I have to do? Then I'm talking to other people going through the same situation and just kind of figuring that out. So that failure? It got me to want to succeed. I had to go, actually literally go to pharmacies and follow prescriptions from the patients to the doctors."

Driving around from town to town chasing down pharmacies and prescriptions took perseverance. Not how he'd expected to spend his time, but John vowed to himself that he would make it work.

"Failure was not an option. So, I had to make it work or else; you know, sink or swim. Not death by fire, but baptism by fire. So, like learning a trade, just get thrown into it versus, you know, having someone teach you how to do it. Just had to learn because there are no failures, there is no Plan B."

In follow up, John mentioned a poem by William Ernest Henley titled *Invictus*, and quoted one line in particular—"I am the master of my fate, I am the captain of my soul." He interpreted this to mean that there is value in resilience and inner strength. He went on to describe that the poet portrayed a defiant spirit, refusing to be defeated by life challenges; a perspective that truly resonated with John.

The combination of being a disciplined child, a learned positive approach, the inability to accept failure for his family, and not accepting anything less than establishing himself in unknown territory carried John through that less than smooth entry. He knew he had to believe in himself, and rely upon his own efforts. There was no one else to help, no going back.

Rachel

There were some teary moments for Rachel during the interview. The impact of COVID still lingers with her. Anytime she talked about her children, it was a mix of emotions. But the rest of the time, she pretty much exuded positivity. She beamed when she spoke of her management team, her mentees, and her clients.

When asked about the characteristics she believes are essential to make it in her business role, she expressed a strong opinion.

"Definitely perseverance. Not giving up. And asking questions and finding out because there's no book to say 'this is how you do this.' If somebody is wanting to start a business or thinking they will wait until they go to school and have all the information and be ready, and then when it's all perfect . . ." Rachel's voice trailed off; she shook her head side to side to indicate *no*.

"Just start doing it. Start, and build off of it. It's not black and white. You have to do the groundwork. Smile when you have a win. You have to have a strong backbone and not give up. It's gonna take a few times."

There were several stops and starts along the way for Rachel. Some were from the circumstances of her younger life, others from personal decisions. Some were from trusted others in the same business who changed course, leaving her in difficult positions. But she persevered, shook it off— and most of the time with that effervescent smile on her face.

Alexandra

Failing at her job would also be failing the kids she nurtures and serves. Alexandra went into her role as teacher, and eventually, entrepreneur, out of a deep love for children with learning difficulties, and it was the way she supported her household, her own children. All of them were depending upon her to persevere.

Alexandra went off on her own to start a charter school out of total frustration with a public system "that doesn't understand, doesn't want to understand." She had many days when she thought it may have been smarter to give up and go back to traditional teaching, or do something else entirely. But she was drawn back each time.

"In the process I learned that I have to believe in the value of what I do, and how big it is. I had to believe that it would happen, that I would make it happen. And if I fall, I will get back up, dust myself off because there's a bigger mission. There's a bigger purpose, and I feel like I have a bunch of kids that I am advocating for, even if I don't know them, because my voice is being heard."

The dynamics of the "system" frustrated her, yet keeping the children in mind motivated her to keep fighting for them, to refuse to accept the determinations made by that system. Alexandra related the story of attending one of the federally mandated meetings that determined what services a child will receive from a school district.

"I used to get in trouble after my IEP (Individual Education Plan) meetings because I sided with the parents. I would be in trouble all the time. But I'm thinking, the parent is right. How can you sit here and tell me that you're going to give a child fifteen minutes of occupational therapy a week? With a straight face? What is fifteen minutes supposed to do—like, this is a joke! Or the insurance company will not approve occupational therapy because the child will get fifteen minutes at school. There's a cognitive dissonance with reality."

Alexandra knew from experience that fifteen minutes a day would do little if anything for students with complex needs. She had times when she felt she had no support, as if she was very alone in this. Times when the probability of failing far outweighed the probabilities of succeeding.

"There's always a ray of sunshine that comes in, and even in my low lows, when I'm thinking this was a mistake, I should just give up—I never do, though. There are families depending on me, there's something in me. I'm going to keep going and do what I need to do to get it done."

Knowing she is doing right by the children and their families gives Alexandra the confidence she needs to keep pushing herself. She did not choose an easy path when she went on her own, but her perseverance, positive outlook, and commitment to her mission spurred her onward.

Shawn

Chapter 3 described Shawn's story of the myriad of errors he made when he started his own company. Those mistakes necessitated going back to fix them later. He expanded on that story, lamenting his lack of preparation for the day-to-day tasks that any business owner must become accustomed to addressing. Like Paul, he finally came to regard failure as a part of being in business, something to be accepted, dealt with, and moved past.

"Running a business isn't something that's ever taught, though. And I think the hardships are what teaches it, all of the failures and, you know, there's no program that says here's how you run a business, right? Because there's no cookie cutter. It was like, when you're twenty-one, you really don't know. I think it was the worst idea in the world to start or to run a business (at that age). It should never be done in my opinion. But that's how many years later when you can say that? You've got to figure it out. Your progressions come as your failures come."

Acceptance of failing, or at least the prospect of it, is something that Shawn didn't appreciate early on. It came with time, with repetition, and by developing a strategy of turning off the constant demands.

"I feel like you have to have the ability to turn your head or you have to be able to turn things off. My early perception of the life of one of my biggest mentors was very, very wrong. From the outside, it looked like it was all the glitz and the glam, till I really saw him and his family directly. You don't know what it does to that person until it's ten o'clock at night and that person is by themselves. You don't even realize that it takes a long time (to build things up). It takes a long time to chisel a stone basically. Every day is adult babysitting, equipment failures, and dealing with life in general. If you can't shrug things off, and just say screw it today, or screw that problem and I'll get on to the next thing, then you can't own a business. You know, I don't think it's for everybody by any means."

Shawn may have sounded cynical when he labeled employee issues as babysitting or equipment failures as every day events. Yet his passion for his business and working hard required him to be on the job all the time. When he saw the realities of the more experienced mentor's life, and the tolls they had taken, he made up his mind that it was essential to accept those as part of his responsibilities, while balancing that with walking away sometimes. Taking a few days off with his wife or taking his kids for a boating getaway helped him find a quality of life that was more sustainable for the long term. That doesn't mean the bad days or failures that taught hard lessons went away, it just means he learned to put them aside to occasionally enjoy the moment.

Jessica

Most of Jessica's answers were not expansive. She did not have the long storytelling nature that some of the other interviewees provided. In spite of this, her perseverance and tenacity are evident from the examples she provided along the way of her progress from the military to owning her own business.

A question was posed to Jessica toward the end of the interview. The question about whether the interviewee wanted to share anything else often elicited a head shake or a relatively quick "not really." The timing of the question may suggest people were tired by then, or thought they had said enough. Jessica's response was, once again, succinct. Succinct, but to the point.

"My journey? What it took? I think it's just perseverance. It's a word I use a lot. Just persevere."

Paul

Paul spent more than a decade jumping in and out of corporate America. He performed the job of an accountant but was not content; it agitated him. When the urge to do things his way became overwhelming, he'd set off to try to make a go of it on his own. The threat of failure loomed around every corner. When it got too close, the reality of a young family drove him back to working for someone else.

Paul fidgeted in his chair as he described the circumstances confronting him on one of those corporate departures. He was still carrying around that desire to have a briefcase in hand. He also wanted to do something else, or more accurately, several somethings. He purchased an apartment building using an $80,000 loan from a private lending company and had a year to pay the seller another $20,000. At the same time, he was in search of a small business to buy, maybe a franchise. Paul literally walked up and down the streets, knocking on doors—inquired at a beer store, some corner stores, then finally, a woman who owned a bottled soft drink distribution center expressed an interest in selling.

"She's like, 'You want to buy the business?' I said, yes I do. I'm also thinking to myself, this is a four million a year business and I'm thirty years old. What the hell am I doing?"

Before long, it was a classic "be careful what you wish for" type of situation. That business owner was willing to "hold the paper" (finance his start-up) after Paul explained that he already had the apartment building loan. So he was working this deal with her at the same time as trying to raise the other $20,000 under tight time constraints. He decided to renovate the apartments himself to get them all rented out more quickly. With the improvements and the space fully rented, Paul was then able to refinance the apartments for $300,000, pay back the original apartment loan, and use the rest to start paying off the beverage business.

Paul slapped his hand on his forehead and shook his shoulders as he incredulously spoke about how he then lost that soft drink business he'd scrambled so hard to attain. Three years in, he realized his inventory was being depleted—someone was stealing from him. Paul had an accounting background, yet he didn't figure this out until it was a dire situation. He scrambled, but ultimately had to go back to the businesswoman to confess his monetary short-coming. He saw no way around it—he couldn't pay her.

Dropping his chin to his chest and then jolting back upright, he described the next interaction—the one that hit him hard. "I called her. I told her I gotta get out of my deal with her, sell it back, otherwise it's gonna be bankruptcy. No problem. She took everything back. So all right, I went through that. Owning that beverage business was my first failure. That scared me. And I almost didn't come back from that. I was ashamed, embarrassed, upset. Disappointed."

Paul had longed to do both the residential rentals and retail. When he faced the reality of not being able to make it work, of realizing he couldn't juggle it all, he was devastated. Just the memory brought him pause; he lowered his volume to barely audible.

"And that's not supposed to happen. I thought I'd done everything right. Every time I got up to bat, I thought I got on base, you know? Still trying to get my home run. I thought that was my home run. So that did not work."

Paul's first wife could not endure that kind of financial risk. They had three small children and she gave the ultimatum. Her response in the face of failure was to demand that he go back to what was guaranteed and familiar. Paul did, but he could not stay.

"I went back to corporate America. After that I didn't go into debt for a while. Everything had to be financed by me upfront. That's a long haul—very long. I was afraid of that. So that humbled me. That's when I learned the most—you learn more from your failures than you do your successes. If you can weather it, you're gonna be better."

A couple of decades later, Paul is even more philosophical about failure. His second wife learned his perspective at the very beginning of their relationship. She was willing to weather the ups and downs it would take for Paul to get to a place where he felt good about his work and didn't have to continue to count on the safety and security of a big company—didn't have to feel the void he felt when working for others.

Paul credits her with enabling him to really go after his dream. "In this business, you need support. You can't survive, I don't think you thrive in any business, without a healthy home. So that was a game changer for me. And that really, she supports the hell out of me—that made a difference. So it's awesome. Yeah, that helped me stay out of corporate America."

Unlikely to Unstoppable

Paul provided more examples of perseverance. The last nine years had tested his resolve, but he stayed the course.

"I tell you; there's ups and downs. There's gonna be failures. And you can't be afraid of the failures. I told my wife, 'If I'm gonna stay out of the corporate world, I got to commit to running a business.' So we've been through a lot. We've lived in a one-bedroom apartment here. We lived in a small town two hours away in another one-bedroom apartment. We've moved around—all in pursuit of today's lifestyle. A lot of people can't see this, but the long game is where it is—you have to trust in your vision. As long as you're tracking, it should come true. A lot of people can't see your vision because it's in your head. And it's tough to trust someone with your life and going down this path, and she was able to do that. Therefore, I didn't have to jump back into corporate."

Failing at his own business the first couple of tries did not keep him away forever. He persevered! Paul did what he had to do to support his family, not always loving his work choices or environment in "corporate America." Yet at some point he couldn't work for someone else any longer. He was not comfortable in his own skin when he was under the thumb of a large enterprise. With a life partner who could tolerate, even embrace, his outlook on failure, he was able to start his contracting business. Start it, knowing that failure would happen, but that he could navigate whatever came with his vision and her support.

Ted

As best can be determined from his writing and his life-long storytelling to family, Ted's relationship to failure is probably best captured in the phrase, "knowing when to fish or cut bait." That expression implies that the individual decides whether to continue investing time, effort, and money into a particular endeavor (the fishing part) or to change course and try something different (cutting the bait).

He faced potential failure more times than could be counted. Some arise in stories from his youth. One that is silly now, but was serious then involved chickens! He invested $25.00 in fifty chickens, with the intention to raise them, sell the eggs, and eventually, the chickens themselves, at a decent profit. Instead, forty of them died within a couple of weeks. So he sold the remaining ones for $1.00 each and went on to the next opportunity—he cut bait and went fishing elsewhere.

As the years went on, potential failures had more serious consequences. Ted moved his business around multiple times—always seeking a location closer to the majority of customers, or more space to store the huge volume of stock required at the start of each landscape season. He rented some space from an elderly farmer and "wished a genie would come along and let this property be mine." He then felt quite hopeless when that genie wish came true—the property he'd dreamed of owning became available. He knew it was the ideal location for his growing landscape business, even knew that the asking price was reasonable. Reasonable, but four times more than the money he had available.

"It got daunting. I may have had $10,000 available, if I scraped things together. But enter my advisor/accountant, who fashioned a financing plan accomplishing what I thought was impossible."

On that occasion, he kept fishing (persevering!), kept going after what he wanted. He used the property for his own business for several years, even dabbling in a retail garden store there. Ted discovered he was not cut out for retail; the hours were long and demanding. More hours than he had available. He abandoned retail at that point, but years later, he and his accountant determined the "highest and best" use for the space would actually be retail—just for someone else to run and pay him for the space.

Ted acquired more land along the same stretch of the Erie Canal and developed something even he could not have imagined when he initially negotiated that financial investment—a street of shops and restaurants. Maybe he had a sixth sense or intuition about such things. But maybe experiencing previous failure and turning it around gave him an air of neutrality about failure. He sure didn't invite it, but he didn't fear it either.

Ironically, or maybe not, Ted's favorite leisurely pastime was fishing. There is something that attracted him to figuring out when to stay on a business path or when to try something new. The same applied to his love of fishing. He was attracted some days by a tenacious (some might say stubborn) tendency to keep tossing that line in, despite it coming back up empty. He'd switch from worms to lures, move from dock to the shoreline, or occasionally decide to cut bait altogether and find something else productive to do with his time. Always seeking something productive, keeping busy—in business and along his beloved river.

Chapter 8

Words to Live By

*No matter what people tell you, words
and ideas can change the world.*
Robin Williams

The title of this chapter was originally intended to be a snippet from one of Ted's favorite quotes: "Funny thing about luck, the harder I work, the luckier I get." This saying not only embodies Ted's own outlook on luck and work, but is credited to quite an impressive array of prolific writers—Thomas Jefferson, Mark Twain, and a publisher from the early 1900s, Coleman Cox.

Ted said it so often that anyone who knew him well was likely to begin an involuntary eye roll as soon as the first couple of words came out. It was such a classic representation of him and his philosophy that "Funny Thing About Luck" was also the original working title for the book. A question about it was included in every interview to hopefully garner additional insight about the phrase from these other like-spirited folks. The interviewees were asked to share what the quote means to them, or what came to mind as the words were read.

As it turned out, no one was quite as enamored of the play on words as Ted. Most responses began with a nod of agreement or chuckle, but then led to a discussion of work, opportunity, and putting in effort, guided by their own intrinsic attitudes about anything related to the concept of luck. Surprising at first, but not after pondering ideas related to luck a little further. Beliefs about luck can originate from an array of sources: psychological processes, superstition, and religion are examples. It would be accurate to say that a few dismissed luck as unimportant and moved on to other ideas. In their own ways and their own words, they each discovered, much like Ted, that pure luck has very little to do with the paths they have taken.

In contrast, the follow-up question, to share one's own favorite quote, mantra, or motivational self-talk opened the floodgates for a treasure trove of words of wisdom. Many are related to life in general, some are self-directed reminders that the individual repeats in times of duress or introspection, and some are advisory.

Inspiring quotes or advice about life and business are fairly clear to understand. But, is 'mantra' as familiar? The word mantra comes from Sanskrit and traditionally implies a sacred message or incantation used in personal meditation. Today, the implication has evolved from being a sacred practice to a motivational tool or reminder. The essence of the traditional meaning of a mantra continues to exist, thousands of years later, in helping humans feel a sense of meaning in their life path. Some may resonate immediately with you, and some may not.

What maybe is most fascinating to the authors, is how many of the words of wisdom shared by our interviewees have stood the tests of time. They cite age-old philosophers, male and female, and have found during their hardest times, that these deceptively simple philosophies—formed into words—soothe the soul, create opportunity for ongoing effort, and become shared ideas. Now—from them to you!

Jeremy

Jeremy smiled as the quote from Ted was shared. "It's a brilliant saying. Your dad's (Ted) so smart. It's true, you know, luck is where hard work meets opportunity, in my opinion. So, the harder you work, the more opportunities you have. So why not follow that idea? He was one of the hardest workers I've ever met."

Jeremy enjoyed Ted's words of advice. His own words to live by also fall in the advisory category. In fact, they originated when he was asked to speak at a conference for financial advisors close to ten years ago. He shared the words of wisdom that he started offering several years prior with advisors new to the field.

"I told them, just do your best, and if in everything you do, you keep in mind to just do your best, then you can't ever really fail. And I don't mean the thing that has come about for millennials where everyone gets a trophy. I mean, *actually* do your best. Your best will get you to the best *you* can do, not everyone's best is the same. Somebody else's (best) might be a much higher level, but if your best gets you happy, then you've gotten the best you can get and how can you want more?"

When he repeated "actually do your best," he did it with an emphasis that in and of itself was inspiring. Jeremy's conviction could not be mistaken. He is passionate that one must be happy with the knowledge of doing your best.

A few minutes later, the interviewer asked Jeremy to share some final words about his path so far. Jeremy related a story of watching his early teen daughter at her martial arts class and recalling his own training when in the Marines. Both taught something called the Black Belt Principles. Principles repeated at the end of every class.

"They repeat these and they become your mantra, your principles to live by. It's honesty, integrity, perseverance, respect, courtesy, self-control, and indomitable spirit. I guess I look at everything I do in life, professional or personal, if I do it with honesty and integrity and courtesy, with self-control, have perseverance and do it with indomitable spirit, I can't lose. Whatever I do, I try to have that as the cloud over my head. It's formed me into who I am now trying to be. I use it as a backbone, a framework of sorts."

The interviewer was struck by the connection between what Jeremy had first offered about doing one's best, and his second comments about principles, and could not help but ask this related follow-up question of Jeremy:

"So, then, do these principles you just named translate into your definition of 'best'? If someone asked you what comprises the 'best' you spoke about at that conference, maybe these descriptors equal your definition?"

A beaming grin spread over Jeremy's face. "Hey, yeah, that's really good. So if you're doing your best, what IS your best? Your best needs to be doing things with honesty and courtesy and integrity and, yeah, that's really it! You helped me pull this all together. That's really good."

Both interviewee and interviewer felt they had made a new connection, a new discovery during this part of the discussion. On many occasions when doing interview research, it becomes necessary to provide the participant with an operational definition of a concept when asking about it. On this particular day, the participant found his own operational definition and a new clarity around a bit of advice he'd been sharing for years.

Angie

Angie's response to Ted's quote originated from her upbringing. Few people in her family or community thought that becoming a professional was realistic for her. The priority was to get out of high school and find a steady income. The outlook she carried from her youth was that luck, indeed, was inherent in finding that job. She had no sense of her own ability to influence that outcome. Her parents gave advice based on their own experiences, so she did not have any framework for setting goals different from theirs, no urging to do more.

"I think that quote might even be my very story, because I do think it's luck. Or maybe not, but my low self-esteem from my younger years showed in this self-talk—'If you get really lucky, you're going to get a good waitressing job.' It was not conceivable to put together a plan and work hard. I always worked hard. I just didn't know that could lead to something like this."

During that phase of her life, she regarded anything good that ended up happening as a result of luck—something extrinsic. So, it may have been luck that Angie happened to see a want-ad for a real estate seminar. Then again, it may have been her own as yet unrecognized desire to do something that really interested her. Then, it may have been luck (or lack of it?) that the first company she went to treated her more like an employee. It may have been luck when the next company she went to showed her a whole new approach.

"The second company came from the perspective that you own your own business. Let us help you grow that business. I had never considered that as an option. And then it was!"

Once she began treating her work in real estate as if it were her own business, her husband joined her. As a team, they quickly exceeded any of her expectations.

"When I came over to the second company, the most I had ever done in sales in one year was $6 million. In that first year, we went from $6 to $10 million, and then up another $3 million every year after."

A series of opportunities, decisions, and hard work comprise the story of Angie's current place as the 14th ranked realtor in her region, in the top half percent. She claims that she feels like she's "still a kid" and doesn't know what she's doing. Pointing to her chest, she quietly relates, "In here, I don't hear that I'm knowledgeable. I don't feel it."

Angie may not feel it, but as her ranking suggests, she has acquired experience and skills, made some remarkable choices, and is steadily accumulating recognition. She currently has a position on the Real Estate Board, teaches classes, and continues to grow her enterprise . . . and slowly too, her feeling of self-worth and accomplishment. Now she may be making her own luck—through hard work!

Maya Angelou provides the quote that Angie shared as her favorite. "Do the best that you can until you know better. Then when you know better, do better." Angie confesses that she rarely gets the words exactly correct, but that the meaning is what speaks to her.

"I use that quote at work all the time. When I do something, and it doesn't work out great, I try to adjust, and learn from it, and do better the next time. That quote inspires you to learn, to be a lifelong learner."

She contrasts that approach with one of declaring oneself done, not interested in learning new ways, new strategies. Such disinterest in learning is a taboo for Angie.

"There's so many realtors out there that don't want to make it great, they don't want to engage in new technologies or new ways of doing business. Then, they are just crabby and mad all the time. I love the new ways, even though I've been doing it a long time."

For Angie, finding new ways to engage in her business enhances her work experience and makes her love what she does even more. The repeated cycle of giving it her all and changing with the times brings her satisfaction.

Tim

When Tim heard the quote, he laughed, then immediately responded that he would say it's true. He proceeded to seemingly think out loud about luck and opportunity, and how they intersect in his world.

"It's an extension of a formula I once heard about preparation—When preparation meets opportunity—that's luck!"

With increasing excitement as he told the story, Tim related a recent scenario in his music business. He was the DJ at an event—a bit dismayed because there were only three people in the room. He gave this exceedingly small group his all, and it's a good thing he did. Waving his hands in front of him for emphasis, Tim shared that he found out later from the shift manager that one of those three people having dinner that evening was the manager of a very prominent singer, songwriter, and producer.

"It hit me that you just never know who is going to be in the audience. It could be someone with access to so much more than I have. That one person could be looking for a DJ to go along on a particular tour and just happens to hear me that night. Never take anything for granted, for sure."

After a pause, Tim continued, "Your luck is your luck. Somebody else's luck is their luck. Some might say that it's 'right place, right time,' but something still led them there."

Tim then reflected on the question about his own favorite quote, sharing that what he uses to motivate himself changes every couple of years, shifting as he finds himself in different situations. Settling on this year, what motivated him now, he said:

"Like I just said, this year, it's not to take anything for granted. The entertainment industry is not linear, it has peaks and valleys. But every time that you're struggling in a valley, it is from a higher spot. You climb to a higher valley and therefore, next time, you're above where you started. You're climbing."

Tim stared out in front of him for a minute or so, more to gather his thoughts than to check the road, and then turned back toward his phone camera. A distinct head nod makes it clear he wanted to make another point.

"I also think it's about establishing great relationships. Vegas has made me think—yeah, it's great to be talented, but at the same time, you need networks, and you need healthy relationships. You just try to be honest and transparent about who and what you are, and you're going to get to the places you want."

One could almost see the wheels turning as Tim contemplated what he'd already said. His next few comments pulled these together, and it is clear that he was far more content with this conclusion.

"Yeah, that's it. Establish healthy relationships with people who see value in what you're doing, and then don't take that for granted. Makes sense to me. It's funny because they're simple guidelines, but hard to maintain. They're kind of the key to survival."

Thinking about the idea of luck and opportunity seemed to make links for Tim. Links between moving forward while being ready for anything that might come along. A scenario or alliance might not seem to have potential initially, but if you brush it aside or take it for granted, it may have been an opportunity missed.

Laurie

Laurie responded to the quote with an expressive, "That's great! If you don't even try something, if you're not consistently trying and pushing yourself, what is that limit? The number of successes completely outweigh the bad things. And, it's amazing when you start to have those successes, the luck comes."

Laurie had a different take on it than others. She focused on the effort expended to work toward a goal, suggesting that once the energy is expended and the goal is reached, the effort doesn't seem to matter as much. Laurie contended that sometimes, good things will cost you in some way, but when things pan out, those losses are no longer as important, perhaps even forgotten.

"Maybe some people regard the money spent on college, or on an expensive project, as money wasted. But, then, if successes come along, those things don't feel like losses. Gotta put something into it to get something out."

Putting something in to get something out—another perspective on doing the hard work so that good things will come.

Laurie acknowledged Ted's quote as "great," but when asked for her own inspiring words, she's not quite sure. A group of words comprising a saying may be good for many, but for her, it was much more about her attitude and the nature of her personal self-talk. She used the example of when she wakes up in the morning feeling lousy or her husband is in a bad mood.

"I will just say to myself, 'What's the matter with you? It's a beautiful day out there.' Or if it's raining, 'Well, we needed the rain.' And even if it's too much rain, I just talk myself out of whatever that mood is, right? And, I'll surround myself with people who are happy. If no one is, then I'll take a walk. I'll call one of my employees who I know is always upbeat, we'll bounce things off of one another, and now all of the sudden, the excitement is going again."

In an email exchange with Laurie after the interview, she sent along a video of herself singing a "good morning" song—a variation on her self-talk. She made up and first began singing this song when her daughter was little. During COVID, when she and her employees could not be in direct contact, she taped herself singing and sent it to them. Silly and simple though the message was—"Good morning, I feel good today"—she credited that little bit of levity as being something that helped them all through rough times.

Ch. 8: Words to Live By

Laurie admitted that it's all too easy to go into a downward spiral if she did not make a conscious effort at finding the right attitude. She considered it important to make that choice to be happy, to enjoy what one does. This translated into how she provided advice to others if asked: the key to advice is to help someone find out what they are happy doing.

"I had one employee who claimed that he wanted to be a manager. I said, 'Okay, then, you're going to manage a lawn crew of three or four people. Make sure they get out in the morning and get at it.'"

Within a few months, that employee came back to her and said that he hated babysitting the others. When she asked if he wanted his old route back, he jumped at the chance to be out of the supervisory role. Later, he found another rewarding position that did not involve managing others and she knows he is happier for it.

Laurie relishes being a sounding board for others and uses her own experiences to look for the good side of things, to find whatever enjoyment she can in a situation and to help them do the same.

Chris

Chris immediately nodded his head in agreement when he heard Ted's phrase. He reflected that his perspective has probably changed over time as more aspects of his work life have come together.

"I like that quote. I think that if you just continue to grind, if you continue towards whatever goals you set forth, more things will open up for you. It's hard. It's not easy. Luck is earned in a lot of ways, by doing what you're supposed to do, continuing to chase it down. I'm not sure if that saying would have resonated with me five years ago, I was still so much in the grind mode and not seeing any benefits. It takes a long time. I think they say five years is your make or break? We're eight years into it, and in the last year and a half, I've started to connect with people that I never thought I would ever be able to spend time with, no less have dinner with, right? Maybe that's where the luck is?"

Chris tapped on the table, seemingly giving himself a moment to think more about luck.

"These connections, these doors open to you. But it's not luck. I've just continued to grind, push forward, and seek out opportunities. And, it's also been some strategic planning. Hey, if I do this, and market over here, there may be some benefit. You could call it luck, call it opportunity, call it success."

It took Chris a few minutes to shift gears from the luck quote to recalling one that he found inspiring. He struggled to come up with something and initially recited the old adage to "treat others as you wish to be treated." Then, with a bit more prompting, he remembered the acronym he uses daily to describe his company's culture, RAP: Reliability, Accountability, and Positivity. He slapped his own forehead to indicate he couldn't believe he'd forgotten this one. Not surprisingly, the adage about treating others aligns well with what RAP embodies.

"Reliability starts with showing up every day—five minutes early. Five minutes because then, by start time, you're ready to meet with your foreman, your team, and that's every single day." His voice and gestures emphasized the last three words—*every, single, day.*

Chris acknowledged that everyone is going to have an off day, or not make it on time; that's part of being human. Human, but also where accountability comes in.

"Everybody makes mistakes, just own up to it. We need to be able to rely on one another. If you're late, or make some other mistake, own up that you screwed up. Let's fix it and move on."

The third word, *positivity*, was one that had been sprinkled throughout Chris' interview, whether he was telling about his difficult upbringing and rebellious years, or talking about workplace challenges.

"Positivity—I'm big on this one. No matter what's happening. Whether it feels like the sky is falling, or maybe it's actually falling, I'm not gonna let people know that. I'm gonna be strong, tell them it's going to be fine. They need to believe it. I'm always looking at the bright side of things. It's not like I don't feel the pain; not like I don't see what's happening. But what am I going to do, be upset? That's not gonna fix anything. It's not a long-term thing; it will be fine. There's always next week, there's always next time. We'll get it again."

Chris's perspective is that your attitude is contagious. If you're negative and grumpy, then everyone around you will be too. He models positivity every day, figuring that will be infectious as well. An extension of the three key words that he also adheres to is "don't make your problem my problem." If someone is having a bad day, they should keep it to themselves while fixing their own mistakes.

Reliability, accountability, and positivity.

Rachel

Rachel wanted a clear idea of where this whole project was going before she agreed to the interview. There was not a clear goal at the time, but Ted's quote was shared with her in an attempt to explain the motivation for interviewing. Rachel laughed and offered, "I have a sign kind of like that in my garage—'make your own luck'—yeah, luck's what you make it."

During the formal interview question about her own words of wisdom, Rachel did not spend much time talking about a quote that motivated her.

"I guess I'd say something like not putting things off till tomorrow. Do things today, because the more that things pile up, the stakes just get bigger."

Rachel paused as if she might have more to say, but then left a long silence, prompting the interviewer to move on. After responding to that next question, she circled back to a point she had made earlier in the conversation. This point resonated as her words to live by, advice that she has given to those around her considering a new endeavor. She encourages them to try things out incrementally before taking a big leap.

"I think it's all about taking baby steps. I've had a few employees or friends talk about starting a business, like a bakery or going into hair styling. I think they just need to start small and see how it goes. You want to have your own bakery? Well, start baking for family and friends, ask them to tell others about your baking. Then, get used to taking orders from people and making what they want. Then, maybe you try preparing it at their house for an event or whatever."

Rachel cited her own baby steps going into hair styling, doing friends' hair in her basement or at their homes, figuring out techniques as she went, and learning about customer service. These skill sets only come with practice. It didn't make sense to her to be learning your line of work and taking on the responsibilities of managing a storefront all at the same time.

"Why start out with owning or renting an entire building? You're just starting with a much bigger liability. Get a little clientele following you. Yeah, start with baby steps."

Many people have no choice but to start small. They may be assessing whether something they have a passion for can even become a viable enterprise. Others may have the means to jump right in, but there is much to be learned from Rachel's approach—not only learning the craft while growing a business, but also learning the ins and outs of dealing with customers, finances, and other employees.

John

John raised another component of working hard when he was presented with Ted's quote. He agreed with its premise, then added the perspective of working smarter and how that develops into more opportunities. His perspective came from many years in the sales world.

"Yes, I've heard that many times and it's 1,000 percent true! Literally, yes. Working hard will get you where you want to go. Working smart and hard gets you further, though. I've worked hard before, and I've worked smart, and combined the two. It gets you there.

John's financial advisor gave him an insight about the world of sales that made sense to him, enough sense to stick with him as guiding wisdom.

"Everyone's in sales no matter what you do, you still have to sell yourself, even if you're trying to work a job somewhere. It's working harder and working smarter. That definitely gets you more opportunities than you would have by just staying home. Instead of just making ten phone calls, you have to make a hundred. You're going to have far more success that way."

So doing more, gets him more. For John, that means doing more than his full-time sales job. He always has several irons in the fire, including day trading, investing in people, new projects, and fresh ideas. Whether increasing his odds or hedging his bets, he's putting in more effort, creating his own luck through hard work.

The invitation to provide a mantra or quote that he lives by was a bit of a challenge for John. Not because he could not recall one, but because he said he has so many. He had so much trouble settling on one that he sent the authors a few others by email later on in the process!

The words that he lives by came primarily from the Stoic philosophy, the belief that virtue is sufficient for happiness. And in particular, he admired one Stoic philosopher who emphasized that it's essential to not only discuss the idea of living virtuously, but to exhibit those virtues in one's behaviors.

"There's a lot of quotes. I'm into Stoicism, you know? So, Marcus Aurelius came from wealth, but he realized that's not all that you need in life. Being a good leader, a good follower, a good father, a good friend are, you know, much more important sometimes. And, then, giving back to people. So, it's important to be a good person, I believe that 100% as well."

Our interviewees, and many of us as well, have our favorite philosophers from which we draw wisdom. John admires Marcus Aurelius, a Roman Emperor from 161-180 A.D. And one might say that his admiration goes far deeper than most. How do we know that? His beloved son is named Marcus. Talk about an everyday reminder to be a good person! Even the word *mantra* does not describe this level of devotion adequately.

Alexandra

Alexandra's response vacillated between speaking of luck and coincidences, while also bringing in her own philosophy about the origins and intents of one's actions.

"A lot of things are not really luck. A lot of things are the result of our actions, and sometimes the results of our actions are not even what we expect. But you need to act out of kindness, love, and respect. There's something in those three words that define everything for me. It doesn't matter what you believe—is it luck? Is it God? Spirits? Whatever it is, if your actions are guided by love and kindness, with respect for both yourself and others, you will have good results, even if it doesn't look like it [initially]. You make your own luck, but luck doesn't really describe it, because it's not really arbitrary."

Alexandra also spoke of coincidences, and the idea of being in the right place at the right time. In doing so, she circled back to one's actions.

"Right place, right time still depends upon actions that you took before that. You have to make sure that the thoughts behind those actions are good, so then you are in the right place at the right time."

In thinking more about her perspective, one can consider the scenario surrounding a winning lottery ticket. What could be a more compelling example of good luck? Except—no. To get that ticket, one still must go to the ticket counter, choose the preferred numbers, determine how many to purchase, and follow-up by checking the winners afterwards. A frivolous example compared to Alexandra's thoughts, but a convincing argument in support of her outlook.

It is no surprise that Alexandra's words of wisdom aligned well with the examples she provided about luck and intent. She took inspiration and direction from the writings of Jay Shetty (Shetty, 2020). Shetty, who has become a global bestselling inspirational author, provides an outlook that makes purpose and ancient wisdom more relatable and easily accessible.

"I love his philosophy of life. We are all part of this reality and we can all put in our two cents to make it great. You are the owner of your own actions, that's all you can control, and you have to be at peace with that."

Alexandra pointed out that this is also the perspective of Sadhguru, whose work focuses on human empowerment. He is a spiritual leader making yogic sciences relevant to contemporary minds as an author and inspirational speaker.

"It's important to understand that things happen, and your actions and attitude in the face of those things that happen will define what comes out of it."

Alexandra put those philosophies into action when faced with a system that disappointed her, that she felt was not fulfilling its mission on behalf of children. She felt she had lost her life purpose, making her disheartened and depressed. Once she saw that there were alternative pathways to act positively, Alexandra found her purpose again, found she could act within her sphere to make things better. She does not hesitate to share this outlook with those around her, to help the children and their families, as well as others, feel the power of controlling their own actions and reactions.

Shawn

Shawn did not particularly enjoy Ted's quote about luck. He said it simply does not fit—dismissed it as irrelevant to his paradigm. Barely pausing after declaring his definitive lack of belief in luck, Shawn provided the following perspective.

"Put your head down and grind. It's that simple. If you do the right thing, it might not seem like it will come back around, but it will. When you do the right thing, the right things happen. That's the model to me—treat others as you want to be treated, and good deeds don't go undone. I don't believe a true good deed needs to, or even should be, publicized. Do the good thing for others—donate all you want or whatever, but do it for yourself, not to get noticed."

Shawn contrasted his idea with that of an agreement between parties that ends up benefiting both, such as an arrangement that ends up being a tax write-off. It was heart-warming to hear a guy who is so aggressively business minded most of the time to be so passionate about doing good things in a humble way. The guy who usually flaunts his work productivity is quiet about his everyday sense of ethics.

Shawn then reiterated an earlier comment about doing the right things so that he could hold his head up high in public and never carry around the burden of having wronged someone. No good deed is for naught.

Jessica

Like Shawn, the word *luck* did not resonate with Jessica. She suggested that the word means different things to different people. She offered another way of saying it that was more meaningful to her.

"To me it's like the more knowledge I gain, the more experience I gain. Then, maybe more satisfaction and a sense of accomplishment."

The saying that Jessica lives by is useful in the workplace, and equally as applicable for her personal life and for mentoring her children. She learned it from her father.

"My dad preached not to push something off until tomorrow, because tomorrow becomes today. So tomorrow technically never comes. It's always today, then yesterday, then gone."

Jessica used this phrase to explain her tenacity for finishing day-to-day tasks while she can. She also thinks it's the flip side of a phrase she's heard others use.

"I guess it's like when people say, 'Tomorrow is a new day.' The problem for me is that tomorrow is not guaranteed. My husband and I were just talking about this with our kids the other day. He said there are so many times he wished he'd done things in the here and now instead of waiting."

As she shared the rest of this, Jessica suggested there's a country song that gets at this idea and she began to get teary eyed. The words are paraphrased, the meaning is clear.

"I think the lyrics go something like, 'You can always go fishing with your dad, till you can't; you can always work on the car with your grandpa, till you can't.'"

She related that when she was younger, her father did not live by his own words. He regretted that error and was now trying to make up for lost time. She is grateful that she stuck by him during all those days because some members of her family did not, and they've lost time they will never get back.

Ironically, much like the "funny thing about luck" quote, "never put off till tomorrow what you can do today" is credited to Thomas Jefferson, Ben Franklin, and Mark Twain. Words that have resonated for hundreds of years. Whatever the source, the meaning is connected with Jessica's father, with her, and it's now being passed along to the next generation. Some words of wisdom endure.

Paul

A subtle head nod suggested that Paul agreed with the quote about luck and work. He made a connection between doing more and luck.

"The more you do, there's just good luck involved. A golfer used to tell me that he had a few holes-in-one in his life. When I told him that was crazy, his reply was, 'If you shoot a thousand balls at that hole, chances are that one is gonna go in, and that's it.'"

Okay, so the more you do, the luckier you get. Paul's story is along the same line of thinking as Ted's. But relatively quickly, it set in motion a recitation of his own quotes.

Rapidly, Paul quipped, "All dads have quotes to share," after which he provided a litany of quotes in an attempt to capture his words to live by. Most were in the context of what he tells his young adult children and his views about raising them.

"I tell my kids all the time that you should 'listen to what people need and you'll get what you want.' The point is that sometimes you need to sit back, don't force things, listen, and see if you can gain access. For example, maybe the guy you're trying to deal with is really arrogant. If you listen, you'll realize that what he really needs is for you to tell him how great he is at what he does. Once you do that, then he might admit that he needs your help to do something. If you'd just gone in and told him what you could do for him, you would have hit a brick wall."

He went on to say he believes that everything between people is transactional, which to him means that business is based on give-and-take relationships. He implied that each person's motivation is to receive a reward from the exchange, to get something out of it. Interesting to note that this is quite a departure from Shawn's outlook.

He continued on and applied this give-and-take principle to his child rearing. If one of his kids wants a car, then his view is that they need to get the job and pay for the gas and upkeep. He wants them to realize that there is no "pass"— not in life, not with him. Whether his son or daughter, once they hit eighteen years old, he contends he is no longer parenting a child. From that point on, he is raising an adult and, in his eyes, the adult world is based on the expectations of getting something in return for what is done.

Mona

The words *hard work* in the quote made Mona think back to when she was trying to build herself up in the engineering business. Establishing herself required overnight travel during a tough time in her life to do so. Mona's focus was on putting in the time and hard work necessary to eventually reap rewards.

"It makes me think of the years I spent with a suitcase next to my bed and traveling all over the country building.

I had to build myself. I had to build my own brand of who I am and what I can do. It was a lot of sacrifice. It was very hard. I was blessed with an amazing mother-in-law who, at a moment's notice, could take my daughter so I could get on a plane and travel to and from Texas in one day, or travel to California for one overnight. You know, hard work does pay off. It really does. And you can't be afraid to work hard—or don't have your own business.

"You've got to love what you do. You've got to. Because when you love what you do, it's not work. It really isn't. That's how I felt doing all that work. There were very few days at the engineering company that I felt like I was working because I really enjoyed what I was doing and that's how I feel now."

Only once did Mona mention anything even remotely resembling luck. She spoke about being "blessed" with a trusted care provider for her daughter. The gist of her story was all about the work and sacrifice involved. Even with the description of the effort involved, the enjoyment made it a pleasure. It's working hard, but the enjoyment and satisfaction she experiences make her feel grateful for how she is spending her time.

There was not even a moment of hesitation before Mona responded with her words to live by, or actually a few of them. She sat up straight and leaned forward with an enthusiastic smile.

"It's all about planting seeds. Every conversation, any opportunity, you are planting seeds. You never know what can happen. You never know, and keep on dreaming. Dream, dream, dream, dream. Do those Vision Boards."

When she repeated "dream," her voice took on the tone of a motivational speaker. Mona was referring to a tool, creating Vision Boards, that became popular for long-term planning. These boards may include goals for any area of your life—career, health, travel, social goals, etc. People even host parties where attendees each assemble a collage of images, words, and symbols to represent their goals.

"It doesn't necessarily have to be a physical board, just know what you want. I put one together a while back, and if I close my eyes and visualize it, that board is the same every time. There are things I want to do, certain people I want to meet. I was in a group once during COVID and we all had to provide one big, hairy, audacious goal. For me—I wanted our products to be one of Oprah's Favorite Things. I worked on that goal for a couple of years. And then, it happened! My sister and I got to meet Oprah. We went, sat in the front row, gave our pitch, and now we're waiting to hear if we make her list. We took all of the products and left them for her, Gayle, and the whole production team. You just never know."

For those who don't know, each year, Oprah puts together a list of her favorite things—favorite gifts at Christmas time. To become part of that list, her producers scour the marketplace for unique items that might tempt Oprah to add them to the coveted list. Mona whipped out her phone to proudly share photos of her and her sister at Oprah's studio. From vision board to production studio, Mona dreamed and followed that dream.

Mona also thinks that since COVID, since it became very easy to work from home, that many young people are too isolated when they start out. She believes that communication and networking are too important to let go by the wayside.

"I believe that you have to put yourself out there. You never know who you're going to meet. I have a great network of mentors that I met through an online group. One of them needed an intern. I wrote her a note that I'd be happy to do it. I figured I'd learn from her. From that, I was able to go to California and meet with one of the biggest natural skincare companies in the world."

Her words to live by boil down to three—dream, visualize, and network.

Ted

The "funny thing about luck" quote rolled off Ted's tongue readily, accompanied by a wry smile and the pounding of a fist on the table for emphasis. Those accompanying actions made it clear this was delivered in a "tongue-in-cheek" manner. In the instances when the listener was hearing it for the first time and reacted to its ironic message, Ted laughed his deep laugh in pure delight at having made an impact. If they didn't "get it," he was happy to explain and expound upon it until they did. No doubt, he would have found it necessary to clarify its meaning for a few of the interviewees. The "luck" part of the sentence most likely appealed to him because he enjoyed boasting about his Irish heritage (woe to the person who dared remind him that his background was more English, for the storytelling reputation of the Irish was the true appeal for him).

Make no mistake, however, Ted was not speaking about luck at all. As was true for the thinkers before him, the reference to hard work in the latter part of the sentence was his true message. Ted never missed a chance to tell an employee, a grandchild, or anyone asking advice, that hard work is the key to achieving anything of value.

In fact, this quote was sometimes blurted out in annoyance at someone who implied that luck was what helped him achieve something for which he had worked long and hard, or who implied that the fruits of his labor came about in some way unrelated to his own actions. Ted traced his views about work to his father.

"Dad's work ethic was infectious, and at an early age I found myself unconsciously imitating him and dabbling at any task, project, or job that could earn money when it was sorely needed. And he encouraged me wholeheartedly, probably weary of coughing up eleven cents a week for Saturday afternoon movies to keep me out of mischief. After selling Dad's strawberries in the neighborhood, raking leaves, and mowing lawns, people came to pass the word that the boy who lived at the cemetery was available to work. It all launched me into a lifetime of perhaps a hundred different experiences at making money to support myself and family. There was much adversity to overcome, and prevailing over it made me proud."

Some suggest that luck has something to do with chance, the implication being that luck is what comes about from factors not related to your own abilities or efforts. This idea did not totally escape Ted. He felt fortunate in countless ways. He consistently acknowledged the good things that came to him from sources other than his own abilities. His journals reflect a deep gratitude for his loving, supportive parents and for people who came along and offered opportunities for him to acquire a particular piece of real estate or to invest in a new idea. Referring to a time when he learned of a large barn for rent in the precise location he'd hoped for, his memoir states, "Make no mistake—I had no lucky charms, not even a rabbit's foot, but did feel blessed at times."

For Ted, it was the interaction of the external factors and his intrinsic work habits that provided the underpinning for the quote. His message was that one starts with what one has been given, the opportunities that come along, and then makes the decisions, takes the risks, and exerts the efforts to make the desired outcomes reality. It's not a matter of chance or a roll of the dice, but rather, the risk, time, and effort that lead to accomplishment. In other words, be thankful for the gifts bestowed upon you, then do something with them, something worthy.

It is safe to say that Ted would have heartily agreed with most, if not all, of the words to live by from the interviewees. He would never argue with the words of his own quoted heroes, Thomas Jefferson and Ben Franklin, when they offered thoughts on not putting things off until tomorrow. Nor would he take any issue with the Golden Rule for treating others as you wish to be treated. He may have even chuckled a bit at the words repeated by Shawn and Chris to "put your head down and grind." Ted's version: "If you rest, you rust."

Ted may not have ever heard of the myriad of other inspirational speakers mentioned—Marcus Aurelius, Jay Shetty, Sadhguru, and Maya Angelou—but best guess is they would likely have impressed him as much as they did us. These words have stood the test of time and resonated with this very busy group of people enough for them to be able to recite them off the top of their heads. That's no small feat. Words from the people who keep the world motivated on a day-to-day basis provide much food for thought, many sources from which to draw strength.

Chapter 9

Success—A Milepost or a Destination?

Define success on your own terms,
achieve it by your own rules,
and build a life you're proud to live.
Anne Sweeney,
Former President of Disney Channel

Be totally honest. When you meet a "successful person," what comes to mind? A stylishly dressed individual, with a persuasive personality? Thousands of followers on social media and likely a great salary? Or how about when a friend mentions that her niece is a successful businesswoman—what do you assume? Perhaps that she has several employees and her company is highly profitable? That this business has maybe been passed down from an equally wealthy family member? Is your first impression, more often than not, related to how much money this person makes, and that their financial status is somehow directly correlated with your perception of their success?

All very common assumptions. In Western cultures, the tendency is to define success in terms of finances. There are some indicators that this attitude may be shifting in the US, but attitude change is slow, and long-held views are challenging to dispel. (Howe & Krosnick, 2017). For the time being, financial status comes to mind alongside the word *success*.

In a study looking at the relationship between money and happiness, it was found that money only increases happiness up to a particular dollar amount (Grumet, 2025). After that, having a purpose in life seems to be the more important predictor of happiness. Admittedly, happiness and success are not the same thing, but there is likely a relationship. The Merriam-Webster Dictionary suggests that "success is declared when one meets pre-determined goals." This implies that something is a success when it turns out well, when one achieves what one wants, something they have set out to do. This differs from money as the indicator of success, leaving more room for individual interpretation.

Googling definitions of success yields a myriad of philosophers, celebrities, educators, and writers weighing in on the concept. In the quote at the start of this chapter, Anne Sweeney, President of the Disney Channel for nearly twenty years, describes success as unique to each individual, to be defined in a manner directed by one's values and preferences. Akon, the contemporary musician, is credited with the following view: "Two things define success in life: the way you manage when you have nothing and the way you behave when you have everything." This perspective comes from a man who, in his own words, believed that business is the essence of life. He expounded on good character and ethical conduct for individuals immersed in the day-to-day activities that dictate business functions, while simultaneously expressing his admiration for the competitive and practical nature of the enterprise.

Our featured storytellers were asked to define success. This was asked at the end of the interview, after they had spoken in detail about the ups and downs of their work lives. Along the way, some had also shared stories about the intersection of work and home life. Interestingly, when asked the question about success, almost all of them queried back to the interviewer—"Do you mean success in business? Or otherwise?" When this question arose, the interviewers prompted the individuals to answer in whichever way resonated for them.

A common initial response was that success is difficult to define. Some even began with what success is *not*. Their reactions made it clear they were not certain of their own relationship to success. However, once they started talking, they offered more than they had expected. See if their views on success are surprising or not!

Jeremy

Jeremy's ideas about success encompass both financial and personal contributors, from practical and philosophical perspectives.

"I don't really look at money or power as success. I mean, obviously money always has to drive you to some degree. After that, for me, success is being in a position to spend as much time with my significant other and my girls, my family, my friends. My girls are number one, after that, no particular order. Of course, success is being in a position to do that, and money helps. It makes the journey a little bit easier."

He acknowledges that with a particular position in a company comes flexibility. It's the flexibility that allows one to have the desired time with loved ones. So, for him, the constructs of money, flexibility, and success fit together.

"You know what? I think success is more a state of mind. Right now, I feel like I am the most successful that I have ever been in my life, not about the money. That's because my kids are all in a good position in their lives with their significant others. And I have my grandson! My family is for the most part, pretty healthy. I've also been fortunate after all these years to find someone that is my puzzle piece, we fit. That's all part of why I feel so success-ful now. What more could I want? Nothing other than more of that same feeling."

As the interview was about to wrap up, Jeremy brought his final thoughts back to the idea of being the most successful he's ever been, and of his father recently expressing a similar perspective during their precious weekly get-togethers.

"It was easy in the past to look at what wasn't or what should have been. But I've gotten to the point in life where I'm seeing it differently. Trying to reframe and think that I'm blessed with both what was and what wasn't. Maybe it wasn't, maybe it still can be—or not. It's all part of that success feeling.

"I recently asked my father at our weekly dinner about his ideas on things like mortality. He always has little nuggets of information. He answered that he's the happi-est he has ever been, right now, at 83. This is a guy who traveled the world for his work—Dubai, Russia, you name it! So much travel and so many experiences, successes. He said, 'I'm so happy now, so successful. It's because I have perspective. As much as I've gone through in life, good and sad, I have perspective now and that's the biggest healer— perspective.' I've really taken his words to heart and tried to be present—and be a recipient of wisdom."

Jeremy's father gave him the gift of perspective. A gift that allowed them to share deep feelings of success that neither thought possible back when his father left him that note on the table to "get a job." Now, the message is to seek the perspective necessary to feel successful.

Angie

Angie's perspective on success originated from what she described as her long-held fear of being successful, accompanied by a feeling of self-doubt about her ability to become successful. She described it as "impostor syndrome." Angie spoke of an almost annual process that she had experienced since she began climbing up in the regional ratings for realtors.

She began her recollection by sitting up straighter in her seat, as if being reclined while retelling this account wasn't possible. Her energy noticeably shifted, and her cadence quickened.

"Every October, when the market slows, I'm sure that we are going out of business—even though I know that no one wants to put in an offer in October because that means closing at Christmas. So I have this conversation with myself. I was always sure I would not be successful, and my husband repeatedly reminds me of how I do this to myself. I tell myself I don't know what I'm doing, what am I thinking? But I DO know. I'm not educated on paper, but I do know real estate."

Angie not only knows her business, she loves it. And she feels that passion is a component of success—waking up every day and having something to look forward to. That, and knowing that her kids have jobs and are on a good path.

After that energy tilt, she resumed her narrative with a little sigh of relief and a smile on her face. "It's not the numbers, not the money, not like a celebrity with followers. I just look forward to what I do every day—I feel like that's a success."

Angie recalled another woman in real estate, one who helped Angie overcome the long-standing fear and doubt of her own ability to succeed. The Rochester, New York, newspaper carried a real estate advice column for many years. People wrote in and asked questions of the local agent, Edith Lank. Angie recounted that Edith became nationally syndicated and was highly regarded. She also fondly remembered that Edith was her neighbor. When Angie was about seven years old, she looked up to this woman, never envisioning her own future career.

Angie's eyes lit up, and that energetic swing returned to her voice as she took us back in time for this memory. "It was the seventies and all the other ladies I knew stayed home, but this lady was fancy! She wore business suits and went off to work, and I knew she had something! Later, I realized that she wrote the New York State real estate licensing textbook for decades. I saw her once at a restaurant when I first became licensed and shared my good news of passing the exam."

Angie became even more incredulous with this next part, adding, "Then, I didn't see her for years. But, at ninety-four years old, she called me and told me she wanted to put her house on the market. She said she wanted *me* to sell the house! I replied that she knew every agent in the state, so why me? Her answer—'Nobody knows our street like you do, Angie.' And all I can think of is how am I going to work with this woman?"

Angie was flattered, overwhelmed, and quite frankly once again questioned her confidence and abilities. How could this woman, whom she had looked up to for decades, actually ask Angie to help her? Her mentor, her real estate hero! But Edith knew what she wanted. When multiple offers came in and Angie presented them, Edith's reply was quick and unwavering. She told Angie, "I don't give a shit. Pick one. I trust you."

Angie teared up a little bit at this point of the interview; she paused to take a sip of her iced coffee and collected her thoughts. Angie shared the realization that in that moment, she knew she had made it. This local icon chose her, trusted in her abilities more than she trusted herself. When Edith passed away, not long before her hundredth birthday, the realtors association decided to honor her with an award. The organizers asked Angie to present the award to the family.

Angie fondly remembered this time, and a sense of peace and calm filled the room. "It was such a full-circle moment. I was in tears presenting this award. Edith had an impact on me from the time I was a little kid. One time, she also told me the story of buying her own home at a time when women couldn't buy a home without a husband. She wanted a place to write—she called it a writer's cottage. She had to fight with the bank till they finally gave her that mortgage. She told me THAT was when she felt successful—buying her own house when women couldn't. Not her books, not her newspaper column, or being on TV."

Full-circle moments, loving what she does, and another woman's triumph over long-standing biases. Success played out in Angie's story in many meaningful ways.

Tim

Tim started his response with the prevalent assumption of money as an important indicator of success.

"Everyone, as an American, seems to have money built in as some part of success—a universal indicator. It's that way because money makes things easier. So that's one type of success."

Yet, it was creativity that drove Tim so far, and creativity that entered into how he defined success for himself. Creativity underpinned the longevity of the brand he developed right out of high school and the inspiring energy that his productions now generate.

"We just had the sixth anniversary of our music parties in Las Vegas, and it was a big success. We sold out of merchandise, released a specialty t-shirt, got a great line up of good friends, DJ friends, and the whole thing was a success. Yeah, there's things that are a lot bigger in the world, but it's creative success. We have something going that people are looking for, fulfilling a vision. Even if it's just one creative moment, it could open more doors."

Creating the musical atmosphere in a room—Tim admits it may be fleeting, but it is meaningful in what it brings to those in attendance. While it is a moment, it is derived from years of experience, years of trial and error. He emphasizes that creative success should absolutely be a part of this book—"should have a frame around it"—because it's at least as important, if not more so, than monetary success.

"Sometimes the little moments lead to big things. The first step to success is doing something—completing it. The next step is, all right, what do I want to do now? What can I do better? How do I keep forging this thing into something that's so me, that I can't get away from it. That's exciting to me!"

Excitement for what has been achieved so far, what else can be created, and what is the next big thing to come.

Laurie

Laurie's definition of success came quickly. Examples she provided ranged from her own personal experiences to those of people around her.

"I just have to be happy with myself. For example, when we sold our house (due to financial difficulties) and lived in a camper, that was a success. It was a terrific adventure for two years, one of the best adventures of our lives. And now I get to spend time with my kids, my grandkids, and my ninety-six-year-old father. I see my daughter being successful because she is balancing her life. She has a high-pressure job, but she takes the time off to enjoy time with her kids."

Laurie stopped briefly to reflect, then offered more about what constitutes success.

"My daughter is living in the 'now moment,' and that's something we've (meaning she and her husband) done—especially since my husband's mother died suddenly at age fifty-seven. We decided then, back when we were thirty-five, that every day is precious. You don't know what is going to happen. Finance isn't what success is—it really isn't. Of course, you gotta pay your bills, and eat."

Another pause ensued as Laurie began to cry. Wiping away the tears, she offered one more thought on success.

"Yes, I've grown my own equity, but at the same time, look at all the people that we actually helped employ along the way, and they're successful. They're making a good living, that's what makes me proud. Yup, success is others' successes, all of us. Look, now I gotta cry."

Success for Laurie was defined by enough financial strength to provide for one's needs, by the time to be with the ones you love, and by the work and fulfillment that the business brings to others around you. Oh, and one more thing…

"It's always been about the journey, not the destination. That's a big part of the whole idea of success. You never know—I'm still on a journey. It's changing. There's so much more to see and learn and meet. Can you even imagine if you felt like you arrived?"

Laurie's voice turns woeful at the idea of feeling as if the path is complete. Success for her is ongoing and ever-changing, not oriented toward being declared when a particular goal is achieved, as suggested by researchers and dictionaries. Even though she has begun to strategize about ways to pull back slightly from her daily immersion in her business, she is not ready to declare her journey complete. Not while there is more to be done.

Chris

The word *success* came up in the interview with Chris before the question was even broached. Describing his journey so far, Chris shared that in the very recent past, he has begun to feel some success. Not necessarily *successful*, but that he was on the right road, starting to recognize that some of the things he'd been chasing were now appearing to be within reach.

"For me, it's about being able to do the things I want to do with the people that matter the most to me, spending time with my family, with the ten people whose company I enjoy. Having conversations with the people that I like to be around. I'm not totally there, but I'm getting close, we're getting close. That's the ultimate. I don't know if we'll ever fully be there, but the more of it I do, the better I feel."

Much like Angie shared, Chris spent several years feeling the impostor syndrome, like he never should have gotten to the places he was finding himself as his business grew.

"I kept wondering, have I arrived? Have I not? But in the last year or so, I've started to let go of some of that. I've had opportunities now to help other people, sharing my thoughts about how they just have to grind. I don't think it's complicated at all. I'm not the smartest person by any means, like I do not have a PhD. I could have never gone to school long enough to acquire one. But I tell people—you do have the ability to continue. You almost have to, in a way, be fearless."

He elaborated further on how things have started to change in the last couple of years. His perspective on looking back on his own experience is now translating into how he advises others.

"I think successful people respect other people who work hard, because they had to work hard. A lot of those things are starting to happen for me. Those people tell me to just keep going: 'Man, I was like you. You just have to keep grinding, and all of those things will be afforded to you.' But, with some educated guesses. You can't just grind blindly. There has to be some risks you're willing to take."

It took a long time and a great deal of work to get to the place where he is now—a place from which he feels comfortable giving advice to others. Chris takes pride in the path he has traveled and is pleased to now be able to share the fruits of his labor by giving back to his community. A recent financial consultation provided another indicator of success.

"Our accountant pointed out that we have donated more money this year than we have ever been able to donate. Doing things like that; starting to go into schools and talk to kids about career options in fields such as ours. It is so cool to be able to do things like that. There was a time when I was self-destructive, but now I really do control my own direction, my own destination. I'm proud to be on the other side of all of that."

Quite the change from the young man who looked at local business owners as "unicorn people" to now speaking to kids in that very same position about opening up to possibility and determining their own futures.

Rachel

Rachel's response is another that suggested the definition of success at this point was something quite different than when she got started.

"At this point—it's when the people around me are succeeding, and buying cars, houses, supporting themselves, and happy. And then, it's about providing for my family. That's success to me."

She smiled as she spoke about her family. Then she added to her thoughts regarding success.

"Having good feedback is always really nice, too, an indicator of success. When people give us good feedback, even if you already know, it's so good face to face. Hearing different people say the same thing feels good, especially if it's spontaneous. Responses to online questions are fine, but spontaneous is better. It's so nice to hear about the energy in the salon."

The interviewer asked if those things made her feel proud. She shook her head and then responded.

"I don't know. I don't like to get too proud, because I feel like I'm not done. I'm just doing it. Maybe when I look back? It's definitely been a natural progression. It's been empowering to be self-sufficient and to be able to do it on my own."

Rachel is another person not ready to declare success or consider herself as successful. She has plans to do more, maybe try delivering her service differently, more in a shared space with other providers. She wants to continue navigating.

John

John laughed, both at himself and the circumstances he recalled, ones that must have been swirling in his head.

He told us, "I've had success. I've had the feeling of hitting the level of saying, 'Oh man, I've made it.' But then, sometimes you start going back down, literally or maybe even subconsciously."

While several respondents pointed out that their view or definition of success had changed, in the sense of evolving, over the years, John's perspective was different. His outlook was that once you get a feeling of success, it is time to re-evaluate.

John called upon some of the motivational words from his own vast mental library of people and literary references. "What I try to do comes from David Goggins, a former Navy SEAL who does public speaking. He says that you always have to find the next mountain, so that even if you reach the top of your ladder, you should always have the next goal. Set the goals, set the plan in place, then commit to those goals. Commit to the goal, whether it's to be the number one sales rep, to make a certain amount of money, or to have a certain car. You always want to be searching, striving for something, because if you don't, it's gonna fall by the wayside."

He provided us with an example of how he inspired this idea of success, a few decades ago, in a fellow Marine. Laughter overcame him and he could barely keep a straight face while recalling the memory. He took a breath, collected himself, and told us about moving up.

"So, when I was in the military, I was a platoon sergeant. First, you start off as a squad leader in charge of about ten Marines, and then as a platoon sergeant you're in charge of about forty guys. As a platoon sergeant I had to do assessments of their skills and their abilities. I remember there was one Marine, he was actually my friend, but he would always just be this kind of a goofball and just, you know, didn't take things seriously. And so I told him that and I put it in his report. He was so mad, he said, 'No, you gotta take that out.' I said, 'No, listen, this is going to be good.' I explained to him, 'By giving you a lower score now, you have only up to go. You know what I mean? The only way now is up and so you know, next time, we start building on that. And that's gonna look better than just giving the high score now and putting you down next time. Or someone else sees what you're doing. They're definitely going to give you a low score.' So, you know, he was my friend, but I had to do it to him. He respected it, but he was still definitely mad."

Then John's answer shifted direction. At one time in his life, it might have been about the car or the money, but now he had a broader perspective. John smiled, as he realizes that while David Goggins had some great advice, it needed to be applied more broadly in his life in order to continue to propel him forward.

"Now, I've reached that level, I can basically do what I wanna do, when I wanna do it. It's really about being able to have your own time because that's something that you can't get back, something you can't put a price tag on. So I have some money, but I have the time too. That's why I feel like I've reached it."

He was then asked if he still believed that he should set another goal, or be reaching for something else, in keeping with the words of Goggins?

He was quiet for a moment, seemingly looking off into another time and place, contemplating this question. We could see the wheels turning in his head. He replied, calm and confident, resuming eye contact like a man who knows what he wants and is proud to share his own advice.

"Now, it's just making people around me successful, or my children successful, that would be my next goal—to make sure they have their right path, that they're doing the right things and that they can be successful, even more so than me, and faster. I wanna do things for them."

Ch. 9: Success—A Milepost or a Destination?

John has reached a level of success for himself, one that even David Goggins might admire, and yet he sees the next goal as success for those around him.

Alexandra

The children she serves provide the first definition of success for Alexandra. This was evident as she emphasized her desire to develop a curriculum, a model that met the children's goals. If she and her staff accomplished that, it would impact the future for those kids.

Her definition was clearly carved from her own difficult path—starting from when she was a child witnessing teachers use physical means to redirect children, to feeling threatened to lose her license in a former workplace for doing what she thought best, rather than just following a protocol. Her words here are emphatic, and full of emotion. She clearly stated, "We're well on the road to building a program, a curriculum that can ensure the children develop the skills they need to live fulfilling adult lives."

Then, she allowed herself to dream big, and described how she strives to replicate the model beyond Orlando—well beyond!

"I don't want to just serve twenty-five kids here. I want to have space for twenty-five kids in most of the cities where they are needed. Nobody else is doing this, and if I can find a way to continue—whether it's me or franchising, or whatever. For me that would be success."

Alexandra acknowledges that building a business that is financially stable, perhaps profitable, and allows her to sustain her family, is important. She recalls with a heavy heart a point in time when she first started the business and was deep in debt—even fearing she and her family might lose their house as she pursued her dream. And while she is not dismissive of the need to pay bills, and feels that financial stability goes hand in hand with an entity that is running well and meeting its goals, it is her goals that drive her towards success. Her goals, considered lofty by some, include a resolve and commitment to making the change locally, and then advocating for legal reform that builds quality programs for all. It is a moral compass that leads Alexandra's way.

She concludes with this thought on success for us to ponder, "When you consider starting a business, you need to really think, what is it that you want? Why is this business going to exist? What are you going to do for others? If the answer is I want to make money, then the struggle is going to be bigger . . . because you need your heart to be in it. You need to have a bigger mission, a bigger passion, something that really motivates you."

Shawn

Like others, Shawn proclaimed that success is different for everyone, and for him, not about money or meeting a specific goal or "hitting it home."

"Success isn't about one day you just hit it home. It's things like seeing your kids run around with a smile, right? You provide a good day for them, they go to college. I guess it's what makes you happy."

The interviewer asked if he knew when he was successful.

"What's my success? Nothing—don't think I've had a successful day yet. But I can tell you I've had happy days—days when it's six o'clock in the morning, the sun's up, I'm sitting on my boat. I'm not mad at life. So, for three or four hours, happy."

A few questions later, Shawn circled back a bit.

"I think that I'm fortunate; it's not pride. It's just the fruits of your labor that can be your moments of pride. But I haven't seen enough yet. I've done some good, but I've gotta see further, see what happens next."

Shawn has come a very long way with his business. He's grown from that one-truck dream to a forty-truck fleet; from mowing lawns to constructing hardscape and providing commercial snow plowing county wide. Yet he isn't ready to announce pride in accomplishments or consider himself successful. He's leaving that for some undefined point in the future.

Jessica

She struggled at first to put her thoughts into words.

"I'm not exactly sure how to say it. Success isn't as much about being rich, you know, money-wise, or anything like that. We might not be rich, money-wise, but familywise, love, we have everything we need, you know? In my mind we're rich. But I came from having nothing. To me it's a feeling, a sense of accomplishment. Like I did the best that I could. That the outcome of something is the best—raising your kids to be decent human beings, having a happy household, that's success. Hoping that one day your kids will be successful on their own. Whatever that is."

Another instance of success being different for everyone, but definitely wishing for her children to find their own paths to success.

Paul

Throughout the majority of the interview, Paul exuded confidence. However, in contrast, the topic of success is one that Paul tiptoed into modestly. In fact, he admitted that when he was first approached about the interview, he balked at the idea, shied away from it. Paul did not believe he was someone that the authors might want to talk to, because he did not understand whether he fit the word *success*. The time we spent talking provided him with a new insight.

"I didn't realize until we started this discussion that sometimes success might be defined by how people see me. Eight out of ten people might think I'm successful, but maybe I don't feel successful. Made me realize that I don't define success financially, but I don't know what other people value or think that they see. They might say I'm successful by what they see me doing."

According to Paul, work is one thing, and it comes first because that is how he provides for his family—"you need to eat." But after that, it's having a support system and leaving a legacy.

"When I was younger, it was different. In my twenties, it all started out being about money. My kids, my first wife, they were often upset with me. Now, those kids live with my second wife and me. She gets it—gets the sacrifice. Now, in my fifties, it's about the legacy. I want to create a legacy for all of them. I've done a lot of things—some things wrong, some things right. I've missed out on a lot of experiences. I want to reach my goal now of creating a legacy."

As the interview progressed, Paul recognized that his family understands the decisions he has made, decisions primarily for their benefit. He declares that finally being in that place is his true success. He values the work, but values his family far more.

Mona

Mona determined that it is hard to define success, and that success evolved with time. She was quite sure she would have offered a different response when she began her work life.

The first thing that came to Mona's mind regarding success was the feedback that she received from her customers. Feedback that assured her the products were necessary and appreciated.

"The customers don't have to question it, don't have to google it. They don't have to wonder is this going to hurt me? I won't use anything that can harm the body. That's the most important thing to me. I love knowing that for people who are going through radiation and chemotherapy—our body butters are helping them. They really love having our lip balm. It's the only thing that keeps their lips moist during their treatment. That feels good. I can be having a bad day, and just get that kind of note from someone, and I'm like, yeah, this is why we're doing it. Every time."

Mona shared another way that her definition of success now differs from what it might have been earlier. In her younger days, she grew up with the expectation to go straight to college to study a profession. She said that she was nothing close to entrepreneurially minded at the time she came out of college.

"I didn't have the entrepreneurial bug when I first started. I was just going to work for someone else. It's definitely changed as I've gotten older. For me now, success is having a healthy, happy family and having joy every day. I think during every stage of my life, it has been different, but right now, that's my success. Having kids that are making, or will hopefully make, a positive impact on other people's lives."

Mona's outlook on success is directly related to how her customers feel as well as the health and happiness of her own loved ones.

Ted

Ted did not often speak about his own success, and the word *success* only appears once in Ted's writings—at least as far as we've discovered to date! It's up to us to infer his views from the moments he has highlighted in his memoirs and the choices he made along the way. Once he found his way back from his cross-country adventure at twenty-two years old, Ted met his early goals and steadily accumulated a long list of accomplishments. If external measures such as number of employees, real estate holdings, and being well-known in the community are indicators of success, there is no argument that he was successful.

A few achievements stand out as milestones for Ted. First—owning his own business and securing an expansive property for that landscape enterprise. Second—developing historical barns in a quaint, canal-side village in Pittsford, NY, into an array of retail and restaurant establishments. Third—reinventing himself as a highly regarded regional lilac expert to provide a fulfilling, late-life occupation and hobby. The one and only time he uses the word *success* in his memoirs is in describing the delivery of lilac bouquets to all of the living First Ladies and the publicity that action garnered. One can almost hear his pride: "When the lilacs were being boxed in preparation for overnight shipping, two television stations, two newspapers, and radio hovered over us. It was a howling success, and we sure howled about the follow-up coverage of thank you letters from the gracious recipients."

Perhaps more interesting, is to hold his life up to the concepts or measures of success revealed by the storytellers in this collection. Assuming those measures are helping those around you to be successful and creating the flexibility to do the things you love with the people you love, then Ted truly found, earned, and enjoyed success.

As for facilitating others' success—Ted encouraged every single employee who ever voiced the desire to go out on their own to establish a business. At least a half dozen people resigned from his company to start their own—including our own storyteller, Laurie. He consistently championed them, promoted them in the community, and remained a mentor. For Laurie, he even composed one of his beloved limericks at the request of her operations manager for an event honoring Laurie. For the employees who remained in his employ, he designed incentives that, for his industry and era, were considered quite innovative, such as expense-paid trips.

Flexibility to do what he wanted, when he wanted, finally began for Ted as he entered his sixties. Reflecting upon the purchase of a second home on a barrier island in Florida, he said, "My lifetime fantasy of wanting to do nothing but fish all day is finally coming true." Not only could he fish all day, but he and the love of his life, Janice, could find the time to relax and enjoy a well-deserved freedom.

"I'd sold the business, had a little money in the bank, and could afford the condo without a mortgage. Once settled on Hutchinson Island, I often wondered aloud, 'Where the hell have I been all my life?' We quickly became fond of repeating to one another both morning and evening, 'Just another day in paradise.'"

While the lilac business brought Ted recognition and satisfaction, the inspiration gained on Hutchinson Island resulted in subsequent decisions about his final years. This passage illustrates much about his dedication to both his vocation and his family.

"One luxurious, sunny day when fishing was slow on the dock, Janice and I began to analyze my slave-like existence under the spell of lilacs in the spring, landscapes in the summer, and selling Christmas trees in December. After all, we were 'retired.' Should we not be enjoying more of our 'golden years'? Was it worth the early mornings for 'the love of lilacs'? I rationalized that I needed to keep busy or drop dead. I pondered another year to taper off, then determined I would rely upon a very dependable grandson to implement the decision. Though his true interests were elsewhere (automotive, real estate, and entrepreneurial), Andrew relegated them and worked tirelessly for us during our gradual 'fade out.' Without his talent and devotion, it would have been a 'black-out.' He had also started another contracting business on the side. Likable, with many friends and contacts, he was always busy. I predict a very satisfying future for him."

All too soon, Ted's years were to be occupied with his wife's illnesses, his need for surgeries on the body parts that had performed hard physical work for decades, and other unexpected losses. They were difficult and challenging times. Yet, to use the word he predicted for his grandson, Ted lived a satisfying life.

All thirteen of our storytellers were reluctant to use the word *success*. Reluctant, and unsure as to how to assign it a definition. Perhaps it is the associated connotation that one is done if success is declared. The idea that when the predetermined goal is reached, there is an end to striving, an end to trying, an end to moving forward. That idea was anything but palatable. For, if one stops moving, what comes next?

Chapter 10

Unstoppable

*I'm unstoppable because
I don't know how to stop.*
Tina Fey

When first pondering how to best wrap up the points of this collection of "can-do" stories, it seemed that some marketing genius at Nike had already claimed the best phrase decades ago—"Just do it." Not to be discouraged, we continued to brainstorm, then discussed the project results with friends. An even better motto rose to the top: "Unstoppable." Regardless of somewhat unlikely beginnings, or the crossroads and detours they encountered, the people we interviewed kept on going—and just kept on going to find a way, some way, any way! This quality made the contributors unstoppable. None of these folks let grass grow under their feet or inertia take hold or a fork in the road derail their efforts. Through hard work, perseverance, positivity, and a bit of risk taking, they grabbed opportunities, went with them, and are still going.

There was no shortage of setbacks or missteps that might have thwarted their efforts. Bankruptcy, divorce,

single parenthood, unwelcome transfer of business ownership, a pandemic, cancer, possible job loss, and probably
more that they didn't share, threatened to upend the lives
of these people, just as happens for so many. Strikingly,
these potentially negative forces did not have such an effect
at all. No one is claiming by any means that the hardships
were a good thing, but neither did they result in downward
spirals or insurmountable barriers. Thirteen people who
rarely, if ever, took shortcuts or an easy path, just kept
going regardless of what road bumps they encountered.
They found some way or another to move forward, never
stopping.

In studying any group or phenomenon, researchers
must identify who they are interviewing according to some
set of criteria—often called *selection* or *inclusion criteria*.
In this case, the decision was made to interview people
who "in spite of unlikely beginnings, found rewarding
paths." Choices were made about who might be considered "unlikely." There was a bit of guesswork involved, but
during the interviews, the assumptions about their starts
were confirmed. Several struggled in elementary and high
school, three entered the military as a first step without any
direction as to what would come next, some were discouraged by others because their fields were assumed to yield
an inadequate income or were too difficult in other ways,
and a couple of women encountered biased initiations into
their chosen field.

A "rewarding path" was not clearly defined prior to the
interviews, but if it could be surmised from the individual's
responses that they felt rewarded, then they were included.
There was no intent to gather detailed demographic information from the storytellers. As it turned out, the ages

ranged from thirty-four to sixty-five; male and female were equally represented (six each, plus Ted, who was in his late eighties at the time he wrote his memoirs and tipped the scale to seven men and six women); and there were two African American men and one Latina in the group.

The stories of these thirteen suggest that higher education or an established profession are not a necessity for a rewarding career or a semblance of success. Several relate that formal schooling was a major hurdle in their lives, that they experienced learning problems, or only remained in school for reasons other than academics. Only two (three, including Ted) found a rewarding path directly connected to a specific degree beyond high school. The rest either did not seek such a degree or took a fork in the road along the way.

Probing the interviewees' attitudes about rewards and successes exposed unforeseen and thought-provoking findings. For one thing, the mere act of asking about success elicited reactions from the storytellers such as, "I've never really thought about that before" or "Until you asked, I didn't realize how I felt about my own success," or even, "It's amazing how your question made me say something I had no intention of saying." Following those proclamations, definitions of success and how the individuals regarded success seemed to be both a surprise to the one speaking and profoundly moving for the one who asked. In fact, until the question was asked, these people could be described as unspoken successes, unexpected and previously unrecognized. An inherent value to the mere act of talking about successes, challenges, and failures was discovered during this process. This begs a question—is the time invested in asking and responding to such questions valuable in helping more people consider what success really means to them? Does it help clarify what they are seeking? Could this type of conversation be a tool to help people recognize and applaud their own successes?

If money or finances were even mentioned in the response, it was only to acknowledge the necessity to support oneself, and then that was set aside while the person expounded on success being far more than a bank statement. As their words tumbled out, they seemed to realize at that very moment that the feelings of success in their lives come from gaining the time and flexibility to be with the people they love, and from supporting others in their quest for success. A heartwarming similarity across the interviewees was a dedication to their families and others important in their lives. This devotion emerged at different points in time and during different questions for each individual, but most notably during the moments they discovered what truly made them feel successful.

Success did not come from reaching particular goals or getting to an endpoint. In fact, if they had an end in mind, no one mentioned it. Reaching a goal meant it was time to set their sights on the next one. Several do not wish to say they are successful, but rather that they have moments of success and they want to continue to create more of those moments. Put simply, they are not done.

Interviewing, analyzing, and writing absorbed the authors' energy for months. At the end of the writing stage, several other people became involved in the process. A potential cover designer listened to a verbal synopsis of the book contents and insightfully offered, "Sounds like it's about people who are like the Michael Jackson song—'Don't Stop 'til You Get Enough'—and that everyone's 'enough' is different."

Not even Ted reached the point of declaring he'd had 'enough' to stop. He did deliberately slow down a bit when he sold his business and bought a Florida retreat. Turned out, that was only a seasonal slowdown. As soon as the first tender, green daffodil leaves were emerging from the soil, he would head back north, intent on being present to witness the fragrant lilacs exploding in his nursery. In the spring, it was time to resume his role as Doc Lilac, purveyor of those purple blossoms. While a couple of our interviewees mentioned a potential slow-down at some point, many have continued to make new moves just since the interviews. To name a few: Mona's company has merged with another to greatly expand their product line; Chris is now investing in real estate; and Paul has added residential construction to his business model. "Enough" is not yet on their radar screens. They are truly unstoppable.

Remarkably, when asked to contribute to this collection of interviews, each person was surprised that anyone thought their story might be of interest. Surprised, shocked, humbled, or honored, they willingly provided vignettes and insights that proved to be far more than interesting. Their engaging and energizing tales ranged from funny to sad, animated to factual. Each person sparked an enthusiasm in the authors. That enthusiasm drove the mission to translate their precious thoughts and insights in a meaningful manner. There were days when the words didn't come easily, but that was not a signal to stop. Like the storytellers holding their own compasses, forging their paths, the authors were inspired to just keep going, unstoppable in the pursuit of the best way to illuminate the road to publication, to sharing what's been learned so far.

So far? At the very least, we hope that a story or two has resonated with you. On the other end of the spectrum, perhaps the stereotype of who is "most likely to succeed" has been completely shattered. But who knows—the rest of the story remains unwritten.

From *The Tempest* by Shakespeare comes an apt quote—"What's past is prologue." This brief excerpt from a longer line is also carved into the National Archives Building in Washington, DC. The words suggest multiple interpretations, one of which resonates here. Past events prepare the way for future opportunities and greatness. By understanding this, we can make better decisions for the future. If we listen to the stories of others, perhaps we can pave the way to better decisions for ourselves and those we love. And, if the decision is not the best, try another. Be unstoppable.

Dear Readers,

We are honored that you chose to read, "Unlikely to Unstoppable"! We hope you enjoyed the stories and encourage you to share your thoughts. Here are a few ideas for ways to share:

❀ Write and submit reviews. They only need to be a couple of lines and can be submitted to Amazon, Goodreads, Barnes and Noble. A few minutes of your time can go a long way.

❀ Suggest it to your book club—and then, invite us to join in the discussion!

❀ Listen to and share our Spotify Playlist. Each book contributors selected a song or two that motivates them, gets them going, or maybe even calms them when times are crazy. Jennifer even selected a couple on Ted's behalf. *Scan the **QR code below** to go directly to the list.*

❀ Follow us on Social Media or the website:
Instagram: @drclarkwrites and @wordsinthewings
FB: J. Collins, Author
www.wordsinthewingspress.com

We would also be happy to hear from you. Tell us about the unstoppable people in your life—we may do a podcast series in the future and welcome ideas for who to interview! Feel free to write to us at: wordsinthewingspress2021@gmail. com.

With deep gratitude,
Jennifer and Elizabeth

What Do You Think?

1. Is there a person from these featured individuals whose story impacted you more deeply than others? Describe that connection and trace its roots in your life.

2. Do you have "words to live" by that help you move forward when things are difficult or that you share with others who need encouragement? Share them and the story behind those words.

3. Have you ever encountered someone and wondered about what their journey was like? Did you try to find out? Why or why not?

4. Several of the people interviewed gave examples of times they realized they needed to make a change in order to get to a better place. Can you think of a time that you faced such a challenge? What steps did you take? Are you pleased with the results?

5. Did the definitions of success surprise you? How do you define success? How will you know if you are succeeding?

6. Have you ever been in the position to give advice to someone else about choosing a career or other life path? If so, what did you draw upon to provide that advice?

7. If you had the chance to ask any of these people another question, what would that be?

8. The authors described the idea of navigating your path with a compass, not a GPS. Did that resonate with you? Share a story about your own experiences navigating life.

9. What other ideas or themes came to your mind as you read about these "everyday entrepreneurs"? What else did you want to know about them?

10. The authors suggest that you TOO could move from "Unlikely to Unstoppable." How could you apply that to your life?

Works Cited

Becker, Gary S. *Human Capital: A Theoretical and Empirical Analysis, with Special Reference to Education.* University of Chicago Press, 1964.

Blatchley, Barbara. "What Is Luck?" *Psychology Today*, 16 July 2021, https://www.psychologytoday.com/us/blog/what-are-the-chances/202107/what-is-luck. Accessed 7 Feb. 2025.

Cox, Coleman. *Take It from Me.* C Cox Publishing, 1922. https://www.abebooks.com/Good-1932-1930-Think-Over-1926/1036870468/bd.

Darke, Peter R., and Jonathan L. Freedman. "The Belief in Good Luck Scale." *Journal of Research in Personality*, vol. 31, no. 4, Dec. 1997, pp. 486–511, https://doi.org/10.1006/jrpe.1997.2197.

Frost, Robert. *The Road Not Taken.* Superb Litho Inc, 1977.

Goggins, David. *Can't Hurt Me: Master Your Mind and Defy the Odds.* BookBaby, 2018.

Grumet, Jordan. "Happiness: Why Purpose Beats Money Every Time." *Psychology Today*, 2025, https://www.psychologytoday.com/ca/blog/the-regret-free-life/202501/happiness-why-purpose-beats-money-every-time. Accessed 7 Feb. 2025.

Henry, William Ernest. "Invictus." *Scottish Poetry Library*, 21 May 2021, https://www.poetryfoundation.org/poems/51642/invictus. Accessed 7 Feb. 2025.

Howe, Lauren C., and Jon A. Krosnick. "Attitude Strength." *Annual Review of Psychology*, vol. 68, no. 1, Jan. 2017, pp. 327–51, https://doi.org/10.1146/annurev-psych-122414-033600. Accessed 20 Nov. 2018.

Jaggi Vasudev, Sadhguru. *Inner Engineering: A Yogi's Guide to Joy.* Spiegel & Grau, 2016.

Johnson, Spencer. *Who Moved My Cheese?: An Amazing Way to Deal with Change in Your Work and in Your Life.* Vermilion, 1998.

Kiyosaki, Robert T. *Rich Dad Poor Dad.* Plata Publishing, 1997.

Lank, Edith. "She's 93 and Has Been Writing for Us for Decades. This Is Edith Lank's Farewell Column." *Democrat and Chronicle,* 14 June 2019, https://www.democratand chronicle.com/story/marketplace/real-estate/2019/06/14 /edith-lank-hangs-up-her-real-estate-column-after-nearly -44-year/1457007001/. Accessed 7 Feb. 2025.

Maxwell, John C. *Teamwork Makes the Dream Work.* 2002. Advantage Quest Publications, 2008.

McWilliams, Peter. *You Can't Afford the Luxury of a Negative Thought.* HarperCollins UK, 1997.

Peck, M. Scott. *The Road Less Traveled: A New Psychology of Love, Traditional Values, and Spiritual Growth.* Simon & Schuster, 2002.

Schwartz, Barry. *The Paradox of Choice: Why More Is Less.* Harper Collins, 2004.

Shetty, Jay. *Think like a Monk: Train Your Mind for Peace and Purpose Every Day.* Simon & Schuster, 2020.

Simon-Thomas, Emiliana. "What Happy People Think about Luck." *Greater Good,* 13 Apr. 2020, https://greatergood .berkeley.edu/article/item/what_happy_people_think _about_luck.

Acknowledgments

This book would not have been possible without the twelve people we interviewed. We are eternally grateful that they gave freely of their time to express their poignant and personal stories, and then trusted us to share their journeys with the world. We thank Jeremy, Angie, Tim, Laurie, Chris, Rachel, John, Alexandra, Shawn, Jessica, Paul, and Mona from the bottom of our hearts. You continue to inspire us every day.

Thank you to Edward "Ted" Collins, whose unmistakable presence has been cheering us on from the instant the idea began to swirl around in our heads. The stories you told us, and countless other people, over the years, combined with folders, drawers, and bins full of your written thoughts are precious gifts.

We are blessed to have friends who listen to our musings and tolerate the sudden changes in conversation whenever a new idea pops into our minds. Thank you for your enduring friendships and ever-present support.

Blessings do not even begin to describe the many ways in which our families supported us in this project, or in the endless list of other endeavors that have accumulated over the years: encouragement while we went back to school countless times; providing loving child care as our children were raised during the same times our careers expanded; keeping things rolling at home when we experienced the wanderlust that took us on travels near and far; emotional comfort for all of the self-doubt that crops up during the writing process; and yes, the much-heralded unconditional love. It is a real thing. We love you and quite literally could not have accomplished what we have without you.

Thank you to Allison, Mike, Ron, and Sharon for being our beta readers. As we read your discerning comments, debriefed afterwards, and then asked you more questions, so many important connections were revealed to us. The final product would have no doubt been very different without your willingness to read quickly and thoughtfully. And speaking of influencers on this project, we'd be remiss to forget to mention the book club participants at Hutchinson House. Your insight and encouragement came at precisely the right time.

To Ed and Andrew for jumping in when a cover photo idea overtook us. You turned the idea swirling in our head into reality in record-breaking time. Ed: who knew way back when that you'd do the photography for this book cover? And Andrew: adding hand-model to your ever-growing list of talents was not something any of us saw coming. To Sarah for treating those photos with care and putting up with us through more iterations of a cover layout than any of us could count.

Thank you to Mary and her team at MediaNeighbours. The guidance that you offered kept us on track, reignited us when we felt diminished, and shepherded us to a finished product that not only honors our initial idea but has hopefully created a manuscript that goes on to inspire others.

Finally, thanks to all who choose to pick up this book, read it, and talk about it. A written project amounts to little without readers. We are indebted to each and every one of you: may you too rise from "Unlikely to Unstoppable."

About the Co-authors

Have you ever met someone, and thought to yourself, this is not a coincidence … this seems more like fate; perhaps it was meant to be? That is how the story of the two authors began. We were two working moms who began our relationship as work colleagues in higher education. Decades apart in age and career but destined to meet, each of us followed the most often advised route of attending college immediately after high school. We followed with graduate school, then practiced in a licensed health profession. After several years, we each moved into faculty roles, found ourselves at the same institution, and attained doctoral degrees. Our roles required research, and we both gravitated toward qualitative methodology. Along the way, we became close friends. It was a friendship that went beyond the halls of academia, allowing us each to share one another's families, common values, and a love for trying to better understand people and their world views.

Eventually, the time came when we no longer worked together, but the connection did not end. During one chat session, Jenny described an idea to Elizabeth that had been swirling around in her head for a while: to conduct a study of people who, in spite of unlikely circumstances, remained steadfast in their efforts to achieve their goals and pursue their dreams. The unlikely circumstances would have various origins, whether by virtue of upbringing, education, or even a passion for a field typically predominated by people unlike them. The study would represent different genders, different socioeconomic status, etc. Subjects would be people who did not necessarily blindly follow the path recommended by well-meaning parents, advisors, or school officials; individuals who stumbled upon a career that even they didn't necessarily expect. Such personalities had long fascinated Jenny—partly because those ideas described the kind of life her dad embraced, and partly because the people she'd met that also fell into that category were just outright intriguing.

Jenny floated the idea of interviewing people like this to Elizabeth. Little did she know it would evolve into this book! So, with her own desire and drive as the initial spark, she made the big ask. Would Elizabeth help? And in her reflective, encouraging way, Elizabeth responded exactly as Jenny had hoped—with a hearty, "Hell, yeah—why not?"

We'd worked on many research projects together in the past, had proven our research skills, and knew we could keep one another motivated and moving forward. Once the agreement was made to give it a try, neither one of us was the type to let any grass grow beneath our feet. The really fun part began as quickly as we could coordinate the steps.

One year later, we are sharing our findings. We hope you enjoyed reading the stories!

Jennifer Collins

Jennifer Collins began writing novels in 2020. A retired physical therapist and college professor, she became inspired to write after experiencing the loss of several loved ones. *Comfort in the Wings, Wonders in the Waves,* and *Bridges Between Our Hearts* comprise the Love That Does

Not Die Trilogy. These emotionally satisfying books tell the story of Larissa and her family as they navigate the joys and tragedies of life. Her books earned Collins the MartinArts Council 2023 Award in the Literary Arts.

While taking a pause in writing fiction, her writing credits now include *Unlikely to Unstoppable,* a collection of first-person stories of people who have discovered rewarding life journeys, in spite of predictions they would never succeed. Inspired by her father, it honors people who chose unexpected life journeys. Writing with long-time friend, Elizabeth Clark, brought yet another meaningful learning opportunity.

Collins spends her time writing and running a family business alongside her eldest son. She does both from two residences—her long-time family home in upstate New York and Hutchinson Island in Florida.

Elizabeth Clark

Elizabeth Clark has authored a wide variety of academic manuscripts and research publications, but this is the first book she has co-authored (Elizabeth Clark (0000-0003-4312-1198)—ORCID). Dr. Clark is a full Professor in a Doctor of Physical Therapy Program in Orlando, Florida, where she educates her future colleagues in areas of her clinical expertise and board certification—including Neurology and Executive Leadership.

At the time of this publication, Dr. Clark is simultaneously developing her first children's book, based upon the lived experience of her son, diagnosed with autism. Her goal is to promote inclusive actions and behaviors in young readers, and maybe create a ripple effect of kindness through her words and her collaborator's illustrations. Elizabeth is currently working on an illustrated children's book, *Colby's Code.*

When not reading, writing, or teaching, Elizabeth spends her time with her teenage son exploring the globe! Their home-school journey facilitates many opportunities for experiential learning in a wide variety of locations. Their goal is always to work hard, but play harder.

Notes to Self